Original title: Roman Battles. The Art of Roman Warfare

© Roman Battles. The Art of Roman Warfare, Carlos Martínez Cerdá and Víctor Martínez Cerdá, 2024

Authors: Víctor Martínez Cerdá and Carlos Martínez Cerdá (V&C Brothers)

© Cover and illustrations: V&C Brothers

Layout and design: V&C Brothers

ROMAN BATTLES

THE ART OF ROMAN WARFARE

INDEX

1. Battle of Lake Regillus (c. 496 BC) – Against the Latin League.

2. Battle of Veii (396 BC) – Against the Etruscan city of Veii.

3. Battle of the Allia (390 BC) – Against the Gauls.

4. First Battle of Heraclea (280 BC) – Against Pyrrhus of Epirus.

5. Battle of Asculum (279 BC) – Against Pyrrhus of Epirus.

6. Battle of Beneventum (275 BC) – Against Pyrrhus of Epirus.

7. First Battle of Agrigentum (262 BC) – During the First Punic War, against Carthage.

8. Battle of the Aegates Islands (241 BC) – End of the First Punic War, against Carthage.

9. Battle of the Trebia (218 BC) – During the Second Punic War, against Hannibal.

10. Battle of Lake Trasimene (217 BC) – Against Hannibal, in the Second Punic War.

11. Battle of Cannae (216 BC) – Against Hannibal, in the Second Punic War.

12. Battle of Zama (202 BC) – End of the Second Punic War, against Hannibal and Carthage.

13. Battle of Magnesia (190 BC) – Against the Seleucid Empire.

14. Battle of Pydna (168 BC) – Against Macedonia, during the Third Macedonian War.

15. Battle of Corinth (146 BC) – Against the Achaean League.

16. Battle of Numantia (133 BC) – Against the Celtiberians.

17. Battle of Aquae Sextiae (102 BC) – Against the Teutones.

18. Battle of Arausio (105 BC) – Against the Cimbri.

19. Battle of Vercellae (101 BC) – Against the Cimbri.

20. Battle of the Sabis River (57 BC) – Against the Nervii, during Caesar's Gallic campaign.

21. Battle of Carrhae (53 BC) – Against the Parthian army under General Surena.

22. Battle of Alesia (52 BC) – Against Vercingetorix and the Gauls.

23. Battle of Pharsalus (48 BC) – Roman Civil War, Caesar against Pompey.

24. Battle of Thapsus (46 BC) – Roman Civil War, Caesar against the Pompeians in Africa.

25. Battle of Munda (45 BC) – Caesar's final battle in the civil war against the Pompeians.

26. Battle of Philippi (42 BC) – The Triumvirs against Julius Caesar's assassins.

27. Battle of Actium (31 BC) – Octavian against Mark Antony and Cleopatra.

28. Battle of the Teutoburg Forest (9 AD) – Against the Germanic tribes led by Arminius.

29. Battle of Idistaviso (16 AD) – Against the Germans, under the leadership of Arminius.

30. Battle of Watling Street (61 AD) – Against Queen Boudica and the Britons.

31. Battle of Tapae (88 AD) – Against the Dacians.

32. Battle of Ctesiphon (198 AD) – Against the Parthian Empire, led by Septimius Severus.

33. Battle of Adrianople (378 AD) – Against the Goths, a Roman defeat.

34. Battle of the Catalaunian Plains (451 AD) – Against Attila and the Huns.

35. Battle of Ravenna (476 AD) – The last major battle before the fall of the Western Roman Empire.

1

The Battle of Lake Regillus

The Battle of Lake Regillus took place in 496 BC, a time of great tension in Latium, following the recent expulsion of the last king of Rome, Tarquinius Superbus.

The deposed monarch, seeking to reclaim his throne, found support from the Latin League, a coalition of city-states that viewed Rome's rising power with concern.

The Latin League included cities such as Tusculum, Lanuvium, and Aricia, which allied to challenge Rome's growing regional influence.

This confrontation represented not only Tarquinius' attempt to regain power but also a broader struggle for control and balance of power in the Latium region.

The Roman army, led by the dictator Aulus Postumius Albus and supported by his magister equitum Titus Aebutius Helva, consisted of approximately 20,000 men.

This force included heavy infantry divided into hastati, principes, and triarii, as well as an elite cavalry.

The Roman infantry utilized the manipular formation, a disciplined deployment that provided excellent maneuverability and resilience.

The Latin League, on the other hand, assembled a similar number of combatants, including heavily armed hoplites equipped with spears and shields, along with a significant cavalry force renowned for its combat skill.

The most prominent leader of the Latin League was Octavius

Mamilius, a commander from Tusculum and brother-in-law of Tarquinius Superbus, who led his troops with determination.

The battle was fought near Lake Regillus, on terrain that offered a mix of plains and hills, favoring quick maneuvers by both infantry and cavalry.

The confrontation began with a decisive advance by the Latin forces, who attempted to break through the Roman center with a heavy infantry charge.

The Roman response was a solid defense led by the hastati, who tenaciously withstood the initial assault.

The principes advanced to reinforce the line and counter the attack, stabilizing the situation.

At a critical moment, the Latin cavalry, commanded by Mamilius, executed an unexpected flanking maneuver that wreaked havoc on the Roman right wing, forcing Titus Aebutius to reorganize his troops to prevent a collapse.

In response, Postumius ordered his own cavalry to attack the enemy's left flank, sparking fierce combat on both sides.

The intervention of the triarii, Rome's veteran soldiers, proved crucial in maintaining cohesion within the Roman lines and preventing a total breakdown.

The veterans, known for their experience and discipline, pushed back the Latin infantry, reversing the pressure against them.

Legend has it that amid the chaos of battle, the gods Castor and Pollux appeared riding white horses to aid the Romans, inspiring renewed vigor in their forces.

The Romans redoubled their efforts, launching a combined infantry and cavalry charge that broke through the Latin lines and sowed chaos.

The death of Octavius Mamilius during the battle demoralized the Latin soldiers and marked the turning point.

The forces of the Latin League began to fall into disarray and eventually retreated in disorder, relentlessly pursued by the Roman cavalry.

Casualties in the conflict were significant.

It is estimated that the Romans lost around 3,000 men, while the Latin League suffered over 5,000 casualties, including the loss of many of its leaders.

The defeat of the Latin League consolidated Rome's power in the region and marked the end of Tarquinius' aspirations to reclaim the throne.

This battle also set a precedent in Roman history by establishing its supremacy over the Latin peoples and reaffirming its position as the dominant power in Latium.

The Temple of Castor and Pollux, erected in the Roman Forum, stood as a reminder of the divine favor believed to have been granted that day.

The subsequent peace was signed under terms that reinforced Rome's hegemony and weakened the political influence of the Latin League, thus ensuring a period of stability and expansion for the nascent Republic.

2

The Battle of Veii

The Battle of Veii culminated in 396 BC and marked a decisive moment in the expansion of the Roman Republic and its struggle for supremacy in central Italy.

Veii, a powerful Etruscan city located north of Rome, posed a formidable adversary due to its wealth, influence, and natural fortifications.

The Etruscans had been rivals of the Romans for generations, and control of Veii represented a significant expansion of territory and resources.

The campaign against Veii was not a swift conflict but rather a prolonged siege lasting about ten years, known as the decennial siege, requiring a massive investment of resources and manpower.

The Roman army, under the command of dictator Marcus Furius Camillus, comprised approximately 30,000 soldiers.

This included heavy infantry organized into legions with hastati, principes, and triarii, as well as a well-equipped cavalry providing mobility and tactical support.

The Romans also brought with them new siege engines, including siege towers, battering rams, and other equipment designed to breach the city's defenses.

For their part, the Etruscans of Veii maintained a well-trained garrison of about 20,000 men, with soldiers specialized in the use of spears and bows, defending their walls with archers and slingers.

Additionally, the city was protected by its strategic location atop a hill and its formidable defensive walls.

The siege began with a series of skirmishes and minor attacks, during which the Romans sought to cut off Veii's supply lines and isolate the city.

The Etruscans responded with sorties from their walls and nighttime raids to harass the besiegers.

Camillus, aware of the difficulty in taking the city by direct assault, ordered the construction of underground tunnels to weaken the defenses from below.

Roman engineers worked on these tunnels for months, gradually advancing toward the walls without the defenders fully realizing the impending threat.

When the decisive moment finally arrived, Camillus coordinated a carefully planned attack.

At dawn, the Romans launched a frontal assault with their legions, simulating a desperate attempt to scale the walls.

The Etruscan defenders focused their efforts on repelling this attack, firing arrows and hurling stones.

However, while the Etruscans concentrated on the frontal assault, Roman soldiers suddenly emerged from the tunnels behind the walls and attacked the defenders from within.

The surprise was complete.

The Etruscans, caught between two fronts, descended into chaos.

The fighting grew fierce, and hand-to-hand combat erupted in the streets of Veii, where the Romans advanced relentlessly.

Camillus' leadership proved decisive.

He ordered no quarter to be given, and the Etruscan resistance quickly crumbled under the Roman onslaught.

Roman casualties are estimated at around 3,000 men over the course of the siege, while the Etruscans suffered the near-total destruction of their garrison, with approximately 15,000 dead and many more captured or scattered.

The city of Veii was sacked, and its treasures were taken to Rome, marking a turning point in the republic's history.

The consequences of this victory were profound.

Rome solidified its position as the dominant power in Latium, laying the groundwork for future expansions both north and south on the Italian peninsula.

The wealth seized from Veii allowed Rome to fund further military and infrastructure projects, and the fame of Marcus Furius Camillus grew, earning him the title of "Second Founder of Rome."

On the other hand, the fall of Veii symbolized the decline of Etruscan power in the region and the beginning of Roman dominance over their former rivals.

The victory also instilled a sense of invincibility in Rome, fueling its ambition to conquer and unify Italy under its banner.

3

The Battle of the Allia

The Battle of the Allia took place in 390 BC and marked one of the most catastrophic moments in the early history of Rome.

During this period, the Roman Republic was consolidating its influence in the Latium region and expanding its control over neighboring territories.

However, an unexpected threat emerged from the north: the Gauls, specifically a tribe known as the Senones, led by the chieftain Brennus, advanced southward in search of new lands and wealth.

This Gallic force was notorious for its ferocity in battle and its disregard for the fortifications and conventional warfare customs of the Italic peoples.

The Roman army that confronted the Gauls consisted of about 15,000 soldiers, organized into legions of heavy infantry, supplemented by auxiliaries and a small contingent of cavalry.

The Roman soldiers of that era lacked the combat experience they would develop in later centuries, and their equipment was rudimentary compared to the more advanced arms of future legions.

The Roman formation was deployed near the River Allia, a tributary of the Tiber, in a position intended to block the Gauls' advance toward Rome.

The Gauls, on the other hand, assembled an army of approximately 30,000 warriors, renowned for their chaotic fighting style and brutality.

They were armed with long swords, axes, and round shields, and their battle strategy relied on swift and overwhelming attacks.

The battle began with both forces deploying along the banks of the River Allia.

The Romans, outnumbered, attempted to stretch their lines to avoid being encircled, which weakened their center.

Brennus, shrewd and aware of the situation, ordered a massive assault on the Roman flanks.

The Roman cavalry, outnumbered, was quickly overwhelmed and forced to retreat, leaving the infantry exposed.

The Gauls seized the opportunity and launched a devastating charge on both the center and the flanks.

Roman discipline crumbled under the pressure of the Gallic onslaught.

Terrified by their enemies' momentum and ferocity, the Roman soldiers began to flee in panic toward the River Allia.

Many were caught and slaughtered as they attempted to cross the river, while others were swept away by the current.

The Roman army was decimated, suffering around 10,000 casualties, while Gallic losses were minimal due to the rapid and effective execution of their attack.

The defeat at the Battle of the Allia had disastrous consequences.

Following their victory, the Gauls advanced unopposed toward Rome.

The city, deprived of sufficient defenders and plunged into

chaos, was largely evacuated, except for the resistance on the Capitoline Hill.

Brennus and his men entered Rome and sacked it, marking one of the most humiliating moments in the history of the Republic.

According to legend, when the besieged Romans on the Capitol attempted to negotiate peace, Brennus uttered his famous phrase, "Vae victis" ("Woe to the vanquished!"), as he demanded a hefty ransom in gold.

The impact of the battle and the subsequent sack of Rome left an indelible mark on the Roman psyche, reinforcing the city's resolve never to fall to a foreign enemy again.

This event prompted Rome to reform its military practices, enhance its fortifications, and develop more effective strategies to prevent future disasters.

The humiliation of the Allia and the devastation that followed became a turning point, laying the groundwork for the military growth and expansion that would define the centuries to come.

4

The First Battle of Heraclea

The First Battle of Heraclea took place in 280 BC and marked the beginning of the Pyrrhic Wars, a conflict that pitted Rome against Pyrrhus, King of Epirus, who sought to expand his influence in southern Italy and protect the Greek cities of the peninsula that had requested his aid against the growing Roman threat.

Pyrrhus was considered one of the most skilled commanders of his time, influenced by the tactics of Alexander the Great, and he arrived in Italy with a seasoned army and an innovative element: war elephants, which the Romans had never faced before.

Rome, on the other hand, was in the midst of expanding its control over the Italian peninsula, consolidating its power after unifying the Latin territories and securing victory in the Samnite Wars.

Pyrrhus' army comprised approximately 25,000 men.

This force included a combination of heavy infantry phalanxes, light infantry skirmishers, elite cavalry, and around 20 war elephants, an imposing and fearsome sight on the battlefield.

The forces were under the direct command of Pyrrhus himself, renowned for his close leadership and tactical cunning.

The Romans, led by Consul Publius Valerius Laevinus, assembled an army of around 30,000 soldiers, consisting of well-trained heavy infantry legions, light infantry auxiliaries, and cavalry.

Although they outnumbered the Epirotes, the Romans lacked experience in facing war elephants and a commander of Pyrrhus' caliber.

The battle unfolded near the city of Heraclea, situated on the banks of the River Siris in southern Italy.

Consul Laevinus adopted an aggressive strategy, crossing the river to confront Pyrrhus, hoping to capitalize on his numerical superiority.

The initial phase of the battle was marked by an orderly advance of the Roman infantry, which charged resolutely against Pyrrhus' phalanx.

The legions, known for their adaptability and close-combat prowess, initially managed to push back the Epirote lines and inflict some casualties.

However, Pyrrhus, showcasing his tactical acumen, ordered his cavalry to flank the Romans, forcing them into a partial retreat.

The turning point came when Pyrrhus deployed his war elephants.

These beasts, unfamiliar to the Romans, caused panic in their ranks.

The elephants advanced, trampling soldiers and breaking the Roman formations.

Pyrrhus' cavalry seized the opportunity to attack the Roman flanks, further exacerbating the confusion and disarray.

Despite the valiant resistance of the Roman infantry, which tried to maintain cohesion and withstand the assault, the surprise and impact of the elephants proved decisive.

The battle turned into a desperate struggle, with the Romans fighting until their lines collapsed and they began a disorderly retreat toward the river.

The casualties were significant for both sides.

The Romans lost between 7,000 and 10,000 men, while Pyrrhus' forces also suffered approximately 4,000 casualties, a considerable number for a smaller army.

Despite his victory, Pyrrhus recognized the resilience and tenacity of the Roman soldiers, which led him to utter the famous phrase, "Another such victory, and I am lost," giving rise to the term "Pyrrhic victory."

The consequences of the battle were immediate.

Pyrrhus was able to advance northward and establish control over several Greek cities in southern Italy, temporarily consolidating his position.

However, the Roman resistance and their ability to quickly raise new armies highlighted the strength and determination of the young Republic.

The Battle of Heraclea demonstrated that, although Pyrrhus had won, the war against Rome would be long and costly, underscoring the formidable resilience and attritional strategy that the Romans would employ in future conflicts.

5

The Battle of Asculum

The Battle of Asculum was fought in 279 BC and was the second major clash between the Roman Republic and Pyrrhus, King of Epirus, during the Pyrrhic Wars.

Following his costly victory at the Battle of Heraclea, Pyrrhus sought to consolidate his position in Italy and compel Rome to negotiate a favorable peace for the Greek cities of the south, which had invited him to defend them.

Rome, still reeling from the previous defeat, prepared for a new confrontation with greater resolve and a better understanding of the enemy's tactics, including how to counter Pyrrhus' feared war elephants.

Pyrrhus' army at Asculum consisted of approximately 40,000 men.

This force included heavy infantry phalanxes made up of Epirote and allied Greek soldiers, light troops, and around 20 war elephants, which remained a crucial component of his strategy.

Pyrrhus, renowned for his battlefield leadership and adaptability, personally commanded his troops.

The Roman army, on the other hand, also fielded around 40,000 soldiers, organized into heavy infantry legions, auxiliaries, and a larger cavalry force than they had deployed at Heraclea.

The Roman commanders came prepared for this battle with new tactics designed to better withstand the elephants and capitalize on the mobility of their cavalry.

The battlefield at Asculum, located in southern Italy, featured a mix of hills and wooded areas that favored defensive maneuvers.

Pyrrhus, aware that the terrain could hinder his elephants' charges, deployed his phalanxes at the center and positioned the elephants in supportive roles.

Light infantry was placed on the flanks, ready to harass the Romans and cover any potential retreats.

The Romans, in turn, deployed their legions in a staggered formation to avoid enemy forces concentrating on a single point, using light infantry armed with spears and javelins to distract and slow the advance of the elephants.

The battle began with a measured advance by the Roman legions, which launched an initial attack to test the positions of Pyrrhus' phalanx.

The Roman infantry attempted to divide the phalanxes by employing a coordinated flanking tactic with their cavalry, but Pyrrhus, anticipating this maneuver, sent his elite cavalry to block the advance.

Meanwhile, the elephants charged, wreaking havoc on the Roman front lines and creating chaos.

However, the Romans, having learned from Heraclea, employed wagons armed with spears and incendiary devices to try to disrupt the elephants.

Despite these measures, the beasts managed to maintain pressure, forcing the Romans into defensive positions.

The battle lasted for two days, with fierce fighting in which neither side was able to gain a decisive advantage.

The Romans fought with relentless tenacity, enduring the

elephant charges and launching counterattacks to disrupt the phalanxes.

Pyrrhus, once again demonstrating his tactical prowess, used the lulls in combat to reorganize his troops and avoid being encircled, though the Roman resistance and the lack of a definitive breakthrough turned the battle into a bloody stalemate.

By the end of the second day, Pyrrhus managed to hold the battlefield, technically securing a victory, but at a devastating cost.

It is estimated that Pyrrhus' army suffered between 3,500 and 4,000 casualties, while Roman losses ranged from 6,000 to 7,000 men.

The consequences of the Battle of Asculum were significant.

Although Pyrrhus was considered victorious, the scale of the losses severely undermined his ability to sustain a prolonged campaign in Italy.

The phrase "another victory like this and I am lost" echoed once more, highlighting the costly nature of his success.

The Romans, though defeated on the battlefield, demonstrated their resilience and their ability to learn and adapt in warfare.

This battle reinforced Rome's determination not to surrender and to continue fighting until their adversary was completely worn down.

6

The Battle of Beneventum

The Battle of Beneventum was fought in 275 BC and marked the conclusion of the Pyrrhic Wars, a conflict in which the Roman Republic faced the formidable Pyrrhus, King of Epirus, who had come to Italy intending to expand his power and protect the Greek cities of the south against Roman expansion.

Pyrrhus, a skilled strategist with ambitions comparable to those of Alexander the Great, had secured victories in previous battles such as Heraclea and Asculum, but at such a high cost that the term "Pyrrhic victory" was coined to describe them.

For this encounter, both sides were on the brink of exhaustion, knowing that the outcome at Beneventum could decide the fate of the campaign and possibly the balance of power in Italy.

Pyrrhus' army at Beneventum consisted of around 20,000 men.

Though weakened by previous campaigns, it was still composed of experienced and disciplined veterans.

The force included heavy infantry phalanxes, light units of javelin throwers and slingers, and a well-trained cavalry.

War elephants, which had made a significant impact at Heraclea, remained part of his arsenal, though in reduced numbers—likely between 10 and 15—due to previous losses and the logistical challenges of maintaining them.

Pyrrhus, in command, was an inspiring and astute leader,

known for leading from the front and adapting his tactics during battle.

On the Roman side, Consul Marcus Curius Dentatus led an army of approximately 30,000 soldiers, composed of heavy infantry legions, supported by light infantry auxiliaries and a larger cavalry contingent than in previous engagements.

By this stage of the Pyrrhic Wars, the Romans had learned to adapt and counter the use of elephants.

The legions were better prepared, both morally and tactically, equipped with specialized spears and war wagons designed to disrupt elephant charges.

The battle was fought near the city of Beneventum (formerly known as Maleventum, renamed after the Roman victory) on rugged, mountainous terrain that favored defensive maneuvers and ambush tactics.

Aware that his resources and prospects for reinforcements were limited, Pyrrhus opted for a decisive offensive strategy to break Roman morale and force a peace on favorable terms.

The Romans, on the other hand, aimed to endure and wear down Pyrrhus, knowing that their numerical superiority and ability to replenish losses played to their advantage.

The confrontation began with an advance by Pyrrhus' phalanxes, which moved as a solid wall of spears toward the Roman positions.

The Roman legionaries, organized in their traditional flexible maniples, began harassing Pyrrhus' men with spears and javelins.

The Roman cavalry moved to attempt a flanking maneuver on the Epirotes, but Pyrrhus dispatched his own cavalry to confront them and thwart the encirclement attempt.

The Romans briefly withdrew to regroup and launch a more coordinated counterattack.

Pyrrhus' use of war elephants once again became a key factor in the battle.

The elephants charged into the Roman lines, initially causing panic and disorder.

However, the Romans, better prepared than in previous battles, deployed their wagons armed with spears and torches to frighten the elephants.

Some of the animals, terrified by the fire and noise, turned back against Pyrrhus' own lines, disrupting the phalanxes and inflicting casualties on their ranks.

The Romans took advantage of this confusion, advancing with discipline and breaking through Pyrrhus' infantry formations.

The battle raged on for hours, with fierce attacks and counterattacks.

Pyrrhus, in a desperate attempt to maintain the cohesion of his troops and repel the Romans, fought personally on the front lines.

Despite his efforts, the Epirote forces began to give way under the relentless Roman pressure.

The Roman cavalry, which had finally overcome the resistance of the Epirote cavalry, attacked the flanks and rear, sealing the outcome of the battle.

Casualties were significant on both sides, with Pyrrhus losing between 3,000 and 4,000 men, including many of his most experienced veterans and several of his prized elephants.

The Romans also suffered significant casualties, losing

around 2,000 to 3,000 soldiers, but they maintained the cohesion of their legions and kept morale high by the end of the engagement.

The outcome of the Battle of Beneventum was decisive.

After the defeat, Pyrrhus realized that his resources and the support of his allies in Italy and Greece had been exhausted.

He returned to Epirus, leaving his Italian allies at the mercy of Rome.

The Roman Republic consolidated its control over southern Italy, marking the beginning of its rise as the dominant power on the Italian peninsula.

Pyrrhus' defeat reinforced Rome's reputation as an unyielding adversary, willing to endure great sacrifices to achieve victory and establish its hegemony.

7

The First Battle of Agrigentum

Fought in 262 BC, it was a crucial moment in the First Punic War, the prolonged conflict between the Roman Republic and Carthage for control of the western Mediterranean.

This battle marked the first major land engagement of the war, signaling a shift in Roman strategy, which had previously focused on naval skirmishes and smaller sieges.

Agrigentum, a strategic city in southern Sicily, was controlled by Carthage and served as an important base for their operations on the island.

A Roman victory at this site would deal a devastating blow to Carthaginian influence in Sicily.

The Carthaginian army in Agrigentum was commanded by Hanno and Hannibal Gisco.

It consisted of approximately 50,000 men, including Libyan, Numidian, Iberian, and Gallic mercenaries.

They also had a small contingent of war elephants, used to intimidate and break enemy formations.

The city's defenses relied on strong walls, siege artillery, and war machines designed to launch projectiles and protect key positions.

The Roman army, led by Consuls Lucius Postumius Megellus and Quintus Mamilius Vitulus, comprised around 40,000 soldiers.

This force was composed of heavy infantry legions, light

infantry auxiliaries, and a notably efficient cavalry.

Although Rome was not yet known for its use of elephants or advanced siege machinery at this stage, it possessed exceptional determination and discipline, and it brought basic siege equipment, including siege towers, battering rams, and catapults, for a prolonged assault.

The context of the battle was shaped by Rome's siege strategy, which lasted several months.

Initially, the Romans aimed to cut off Agrigentum's supply lines and weaken its defenders through starvation.

The Carthaginian forces in the city, under the command of Hannibal Gisco, resisted tenaciously, using their knowledge of the terrain and the high morale of their well-trained mercenaries.

However, as time passed, the situation in the city grew desperate as resources dwindled and pressure from the Roman army increased.

Hanno, leading a Carthaginian relief army, arrived with the objective of breaking the Roman siege and relieving Agrigentum.

He brought additional forces, including a Numidian cavalry renowned for its mobility and skirmishing capabilities.

Informed of Hanno's arrival, the Romans reinforced their positions and prepared for a pitched battle.

The engagement began with maneuvers by the Carthaginian cavalry, aiming to destabilize the Roman lines through rapid attacks and skirmishes.

However, the Roman cavalry, supported by light infantry, managed to repel the initial attacks, holding their positions and minimizing casualties.

Hanno's main advance collided with the Roman infantry in a frontal engagement.

The Carthaginian tactic of using war elephants to break the Roman lines had an initial impact, but the Roman legions' experience in maintaining cohesion under critical conditions allowed them to withstand the assault.

The legionaries, armed with pilum and gladius swords, launched a coordinated counterattack, targeting the flanks and exploiting any openings in the enemy formation.

The assault continued for hours, and fatigue began to affect the effectiveness of both sides.

Despite their efforts, the Carthaginians found themselves encircled as the Romans used their discipline and phalanx formation to advance and divide the enemy.

The tactical skill of the Roman consuls allowed for a final coordinated strike that broke the Carthaginian lines.

Seeing the situation was untenable, Hanno ordered a retreat to save as many of his forces as possible.

Even so, Carthaginian losses were heavy, with approximately 10,000 men killed or captured, while the Romans also suffered between 3,000 and 4,000 casualties.

The siege culminated in the Roman capture of Agrigentum.

The remaining defenders, led by Hannibal Gisco, attempted to flee under the cover of darkness, but many were intercepted and captured.

The city fell into Roman hands, and its sack provided a significant moral and material boost for Rome.

The victory demonstrated Rome's ability to conduct prolonged campaigns and laid the foundation for its dominance in Sicily, weakening Carthage's presence in the region.

The fall of Agrigentum also sent a clear message to other Greek cities and allies in Sicily, showcasing Rome's determination and its capability to challenge the powerful Carthaginians on land.

8

The Battle of the Aegates Islands

The Battle of the Aegates Islands, fought in 241 BC, marked the climax and conclusion of the First Punic War, a 23-year conflict between the Roman Republic and Carthage for control of the western Mediterranean.

The war, characterized by intense naval and land battles, had pushed both powers to the limits of their economic and military resources.

For years, Rome had struggled to establish its dominance in Sicily and disrupt Carthaginian supply routes, while Carthage sought to maintain its strongholds on the island and protect its commercial and territorial interests.

The battle's context centered on Carthage's final attempt to maintain its hold on Sicily.

With control of the city of Lilybaeum and other strategic positions still in their hands, the Carthaginians, led by naval commander Hanno, were prepared to send a convoy of reinforcements and supplies to their forces on the island.

Rome, aware of the critical importance of this convoy, had rebuilt its fleet after a disastrous shipwreck in previous years.

Roman Consul Gaius Lutatius Catulus commanded the renewed navy, which was better equipped and manned by experienced sailors.

The Roman fleet consisted of approximately 200 quinqueremes, ships designed for speed and close combat, equipped with reinforced rams to strike enemy vessels.

The Romans had introduced improvements in their boarding techniques, building on experience gained in previous battles and using the corvus when necessary.

The Carthaginian fleet, under Hanno, comprised around 250 ships, including triremes and quinqueremes.

However, due to the urgency of protecting the supply convoy, many of these ships were manned by less experienced sailors and rowers.

The engagement took place off the Aegates Islands, an archipelago west of Sicily, on March 10, 241 BC.

The Romans, well-informed about the Carthaginian fleet's route thanks to their scouting network, chose a strategic position aided by favorable winds.

Gaius Lutatius Catulus, who had carefully planned the attack, waited for the Carthaginians to approach in a convoy protection formation, with warships escorting the supply vessels.

When the battle began, the Romans capitalized on their wind advantage and struck hard at the Carthaginian vanguard.

The lighter, more maneuverable Roman ships broke through the enemy's defensive lines, using their rams to smash the hulls of Carthaginian vessels.

Boarding tactics allowed Roman legionaries to move from ship to ship, engaging in close combat and seizing control of several enemy vessels.

The inexperience of the Carthaginian sailors became evident when their defensive formation broke, and many ships descended into chaos as they attempted to evade the Romans.

Commander Hanno tried to reorganize his forces and launch a counterattack to protect the convoy, but the coordination of the Roman fleet and the tactical superiority of Catulus rendered his efforts futile.

The Roman maneuvers involved encircling the Carthaginian ships attempting to flee, ensuring that the supply convoy could not reach Sicily.

The battle was brutal and prolonged, with significant casualties on both sides.

Carthage lost over 50 ships sunk, and around 70 were captured along with their crews.

Human losses are estimated in the thousands, with many Carthaginian sailors and soldiers either killed or captured.

The Romans suffered comparatively fewer losses, with only a few dozen ships damaged and several hundred casualties among sailors and legionaries.

However, they managed to maintain cohesion and continued fighting effectively.

The battle proved decisive, as the destruction of the Carthaginian fleet and the capture of much of the supply convoy dealt a fatal blow to Carthaginian resistance in Sicily.

With no ability to reinforce or resupply, Carthage was forced to negotiate peace.

The First Punic War ended with the signing of a treaty in which Carthage ceded Sicily to Rome and agreed to pay a significant war indemnity.

This victory not only consolidated Roman control over the island but also marked the beginning of Rome's expansion beyond the Italian peninsula, laying the groundwork for its future hegemony in the western Mediterranean.

The defeat, on the other hand, ushered in a period of internal and financial difficulties for Carthage, which would later lead to a second, even more ferocious, conflict between the two powers.

9

The Battle of the Trebia

Fought in 218 BC, it was one of the earliest and most significant engagements of the Second Punic War, in which Rome faced the formidable Carthaginian general Hannibal Barca.

This conflict arose after Hannibal, in a bold and famous campaign, crossed the Alps with his army and war elephants, surprising Rome by bringing the war to the heart of the Italian peninsula.

Tension in Rome was palpable; the Republic, unprepared for such a daring and swift incursion, mobilized its legions under the command of Consul Tiberius Sempronius Longus, who hastened to confront the enemy.

Hannibal's Carthaginian army consisted of approximately 40,000 men, including heavy infantry composed of Libyan, Numidian, Iberian, and Gallic mercenaries, and a highly effective cavalry known for its speed and combat prowess.

This cavalry included Numidian horsemen renowned for their skirmishing tactics and rapid maneuvers.

Additionally, the army had a small contingent of war elephants which, though weakened by the arduous Alpine crossing, still posed a psychological and tactical threat on the battlefield.

Hannibal, celebrated for his strategic brilliance, devised a plan to lure the Roman army into a trap, exploiting the terrain and the harsh winter conditions.

The Roman army under Tiberius Sempronius Longus consisted of approximately 42,000 men, comprising several legions of heavy infantry, auxiliaries, and a cavalry force far smaller than Hannibal's.

Confident and eager to secure a quick victory that would bolster his position and prestige in Rome, Sempronius was willing to engage even under adverse conditions.

The Roman army also included allied Italian troops, which bolstered the legionary formations, but it lacked the mobility and training that characterized the Carthaginian cavalry.

The battle unfolded on the icy banks of the Trebia River, in the region of modern-day Emilia-Romagna.

Hannibal had chosen this terrain with precision, using the river as a natural obstacle to hinder Roman movement.

In the days leading up to the battle, Carthaginian forces employed guerrilla tactics and harassment to weaken Roman morale and endurance, depleting their supplies.

Observing Sempronius' eagerness, Hannibal meticulously prepared an ambush.

On the morning of the battle, Hannibal sent his brother Mago with an elite force of light infantry and cavalry to hide in a depression on the edge of the battlefield, ready to strike from the flank.

Meanwhile, the Numidian cavalry and skirmishers launched attacks on the Roman vanguard, provoking the legions and luring them onto the frozen, slippery ground of the Trebia River.

Sempronius, eager to prove his capability and unaware of the ambush, ordered his troops to cross the icy river.

The Roman forces, soaked and weakened by the cold, emerged on the other side in a disorganized formation.

Hannibal seized the opportunity, launching his cavalry against the Roman flanks while his heavy infantry advanced in the center.

The outnumbered Roman cavalry was quickly overwhelmed and scattered, leaving the legions exposed on the flanks.

At this critical moment, Mago and his hidden force emerged from the depression and attacked the Romans from the rear, completing the trap.

The legionaries, caught in a perfect ambush, fought bravely, but the lack of coordination and the element of surprise made their resistance futile.

The Carthaginians delivered a devastating blow, using spears, short swords, and the ferocity of their elephants to sow chaos.

Roman casualties were significant; an estimated 25,000 soldiers were killed or captured, while the Carthaginians suffered lighter but still considerable losses of between 5,000 and 10,000 men.

The surviving legions, battered and demoralized, managed to retreat with the help of a small unit that maintained discipline under the command of junior officers, but the outcome was a clear victory for Hannibal.

The immediate consequence of the battle was a severe blow to Roman morale and further confirmation of Hannibal's military genius.

The Carthaginian demonstrated his ability to defeat the Romans on their own territory by employing superior strategic tactics.

The victory at Trebia solidified Hannibal's presence in northern Italy and allowed him to advance further south, spreading fear among the Roman population and forcing the Republic to reconsider its strategy for the coming years of the war.

The battle also marked the beginning of a series of Roman defeats, culminating in the disaster at Cannae two years later.

10

The Battle of Lake Trasimene

The Battle of Lake Trasimene occurred in 217 BC and was one of Hannibal Barca's most remarkable victories during the Second Punic War, showcasing his tactical genius.

Following his audacious crossing of the Alps and his victory at the Battle of Trebia, Hannibal had secured a strong position in northern Italy.

Alarmed by the Carthaginian army's advance and continued defeats, Rome mobilized a new army under the command of Consul Gaius Flaminius Nepos.

Flaminius, known for his bravery but also for his impulsiveness, sought to halt Hannibal's advance and restore Roman honor.

The Carthaginian army consisted of approximately 40,000 men, including light and Iberian infantry, Libyan heavy infantry, Numidian cavalry, and a contingent of war elephants.

However, by this time, the number of elephants had significantly dwindled due to losses during the Alpine crossing.

The Carthaginian cavalry, led by Hannibal's brother Mago, was particularly feared for its skill in maneuver warfare and ambushes.

Hannibal had already demonstrated his strategic expertise and deep understanding of military psychology, adept at exploiting his enemies' weaknesses and leveraging the terrain to his advantage.

The Roman army under Flaminius consisted of about 30,000 troops, mostly heavy infantry legionaries, with a limited number of cavalry.

The Romans were determined to confront Hannibal directly, and in his eagerness to intercept him, Flaminius allowed himself to be driven by his desire for battle without fully assessing the strategic situation—a mistake Hannibal was ready to exploit.

Flaminius and his men marched north, following Hannibal's movements, as Hannibal employed diversionary tactics to lure the consul into a disadvantageous position.

The terrain Hannibal chose for the ambush was a narrow strip of land between Lake Trasimene and steep hills—a location that severely restricted an army's maneuverability.

On the eve of the battle, Hannibal concealed his troops in the wooded hills around the lake, giving them precise orders to attack at his signal.

Mago and the cavalry were positioned on the flanks to cut off any attempt at retreat.

On the morning of the battle, a thick fog blanketed the area, making it even more difficult for the Romans to detect the enemy's deployment.

Confident that Hannibal was retreating and not anticipating an ambush, Flaminius ordered his troops to advance without adopting a defensive formation.

Once the Romans were completely trapped in the narrow pass, Hannibal gave the signal, and the Carthaginians surged down from the hills like an unstoppable tide.

The surprise was absolute.

The Carthaginian cavalry charged from the flanks, cutting off escape routes, while the infantry attacked fiercely from the heights.

Panic seized the Roman legionaries.

Amid the chaos, men pushed each other toward the lake, where many drowned while trying to escape.

Flaminius, who fought bravely to reorganize his troops, was surrounded and killed by a Carthaginian infantry unit.

The battle, more a massacre than a confrontation, saw the demoralized Romans, with no room to maneuver, slaughtered mercilessly.

Roman casualties were devastating, with an estimated 15,000 men killed in the battle, and another 10,000 captured or scattered in the surrounding area.

Carthaginian losses were far lighter, with around 2,500 men killed, mostly in the fiercest infantry engagements.

Mago's cavalry played a crucial role in sealing the victory by preventing the escape of surviving Romans.

The immediate consequence of the battle was a collapse in Roman morale and a sense of vulnerability not felt since the Gallic invasion a century earlier.

In response to the gravity of the defeat, the Roman Senate appointed the experienced general Quintus Fabius Maximus as dictator.

He adopted a strategy of attrition, avoiding direct engagements with Hannibal—a strategy later known as the "Fabian" approach.

11

The Battle of Cannae

The Battle of Cannae, fought on August 2, 216 BC, is remembered as one of the greatest tactical victories in military history and a remarkable example of Hannibal Barca's strategic genius.

This battle occurred in the context of the Second Punic War, a conflict between Rome and Carthage for control of the western Mediterranean.

Following Hannibal's series of initial successes, including decisive victories at Trebia and Lake Trasimene, Rome was determined to halt his devastating campaign on Italian soil.

The Roman army, commanded by Consuls Lucius Aemilius Paullus and Gaius Terentius Varro, was a massive force of approximately 86,000 soldiers.

This included heavy infantry legions, light infantry, and around 6,000 cavalry.

The Romans relied on their renowned discipline and phalanx formation to overwhelm the enemy.

In contrast, Hannibal led an army of about 50,000 men, a diverse mix of forces including Libyan heavy infantry, Iberian and Gallic warriors, and a formidable cavalry composed mainly of Numidian and Celtic horsemen, renowned for their agility and combat prowess.

The choice of the battlefield at Cannae was Hannibal's doing, as he deliberately sought an open and flat space near the River Aufidus (Ofanto).

The layout of the terrain, with the river limiting the Roman retreat and the warm southeastern winds blowing sand into the Roman ranks, gave Hannibal a crucial tactical advantage.

The Romans, confident in their numerical superiority, sought a decisive confrontation, disregarding warnings about Hannibal's cunning.

Hannibal arranged his troops in an unusual crescent-shaped formation, with the lighter Gauls and Iberians positioned at the front, forming the center of the line, while the more disciplined and better-equipped Libyan infantry were placed on the flanks.

This formation was designed to lure the Romans toward the center, where they would be enveloped by the Carthaginian flanks.

The cavalry, led by the Numidians under Maharbal and the Celts, was deployed on both ends of the army.

On the day of the battle, Varro, who held command at the time, ordered a massive frontal advance, relying on the strength of the Roman heavy infantry to break Hannibal's center.

The Romans advanced in such dense formation that their maneuverability was compromised.

As the legions pushed forward, the Carthaginian center, composed of Gallic and Iberian warriors, deliberately began to give way, drawing the Romans deeper into an increasingly narrow trap.

Once the Romans were fully committed to the center of the crescent, Hannibal's Libyan flanks, which had remained relatively inactive until then, pivoted and attacked the Romans from the sides, closing the formation like a pair of giant doors.

Meanwhile, the Carthaginian cavalry, having swept away the Roman horsemen on the flanks, returned to attack the Roman forces from the rear.

The Romans, trapped in a complete encirclement, found themselves unable to move or fight effectively.

The result was a massacre.

Over the next several hours, the Roman legions were annihilated in desperate combat.

The lack of space and the relentless pressure from the Carthaginian forces caused the Roman lines to collapse, and Hannibal's army carried out a systematic slaughter.

Of the approximately 86,000 Roman soldiers, it is estimated that between 50,000 and 70,000 were killed on the battlefield, including Consul Aemilius Paullus and many other high-ranking officers.

Carthaginian losses, by comparison, were modest, estimated at around 5,700 men, mostly from the center that had absorbed the initial impact of the Roman infantry.

The consequences of the Battle of Cannae were devastating for Rome.

News of the defeat shook the Republic to its core.

Several Italian allies, previously loyal to Rome, began to doubt its power and defected to Hannibal's side.

However, instead of surrendering or seeking a settlement, Rome adopted a policy of total resistance, supported by the war of attrition strategy implemented by Dictator Quintus Fabius Maximus.

Cannae became an immortal lesson in military history on the

use of the double envelopment tactic, a feat that solidified Hannibal as one of the greatest strategists in history.

However, despite his success, he was never able to capture the city of Rome or force its surrender.

12

The Battle of Zama

The Battle of Zama took place in 202 BC and marked the climax of the Second Punic War, a conflict that had lasted over 16 years and pitted Rome against Carthage in a struggle for supremacy in the western Mediterranean.

After Hannibal's remarkable series of victories in Italy, including Trebia, Lake Trasimene, and Cannae, Rome shifted its strategy and brought the war to Carthage's own territory.

Publius Cornelius Scipio, known as Scipio Africanus for his achievements in Africa, was tasked with leading this risky campaign.

Both armies arrived at Zama with well-trained and highly motivated forces.

Scipio commanded approximately 35,000 soldiers, primarily composed of experienced Roman legions and a contingent of allied Numidian troops under King Masinissa, whose defection from Carthage to Rome would prove crucial.

The Roman infantry was organized in their traditional manipular formations, known for their flexibility on the battlefield, and also included a cavalry force of around 6,000 men, significantly bolstered by the Numidian horsemen, renowned for their speed and agility.

Hannibal, on the other hand, assembled an army of about 50,000 men.

This army included very few veterans, so the troops largely lacked combat experience.

It consisted of Carthaginian soldiers, Gallic and Iberian mercenaries, African infantry, and a contingent of war elephants, a symbol of Carthaginian power.

The Carthaginian cavalry, however, was weaker, as the Numidians who once fought alongside Hannibal were now allied with Scipio.

Hannibal personally led his forces, and despite the clear disadvantage in cavalry, he relied on his tactical genius to neutralize the Roman advantage.

On the day of the battle, the two armies faced off on the arid plain of Zama.

Hannibal deployed his elephants at the front, intending to break through the Roman lines and sow chaos.

Behind them, he positioned his mercenary infantry, followed by a second line of African and Libyan troops, and a third line made up of his most experienced veterans—those who had survived the brutal campaigns in Italy.

Scipio, aware of the threat posed by the elephants, arranged his legions in lines with wide gaps between them to allow the elephants to pass through without causing destruction.

The battle began with the charge of the elephants, accompanied by the thunder of drums and war cries aimed at intimidating the Roman troops.

However, Scipio's soldiers stood firm, responding by blowing trumpets and hurling javelins to frighten the elephants.

Many of the elephants, disoriented and terrified, veered toward the flanks, where Masinissa's Numidian cavalry and the Roman horsemen engaged and scattered them, causing havoc among the Carthaginian cavalry accompanying the animals.

The Carthaginian infantry advanced upon seeing the disorderly retreat of the elephants.

The mercenaries, eager to prove their worth, attacked fiercely but were met with the disciplined resistance of the Roman maniples.

The fighting was intense, and the Carthaginian mercenaries managed to push back the Roman front lines.

However, the lack of cohesion and support from the Carthaginian second line prevented a decisive breakthrough.

As the mercenaries began to fall back, Hannibal ordered his African troops to advance to maintain pressure, but this caused confusion and clashes within the Carthaginian ranks.

Scipio capitalized on the disarray and ordered his forces to advance in a coordinated effort.

The Roman maniples pressed forward, breaking through the Carthaginian lines.

Meanwhile, Masinissa and the Roman cavalry, having defeated the Carthaginian cavalry, returned to the battlefield and attacked the Carthaginian rear.

Surrounded and with no avenue of retreat, Hannibal's army was forced into desperate fighting.

The third line, composed of Hannibal's veterans, resisted tenaciously but could not turn the tide of the battle.

The battle ended in a decisive defeat for Carthage.

Roman casualties were moderate in comparison, with around 4,000 dead and wounded, while Carthaginian losses were estimated at over 20,000 killed and captured.

Recognizing the inevitable defeat, Hannibal managed to escape the battlefield and retreated to Carthage, where he advocated for surrender.

The consequences of the Battle of Zama were monumental.

Carthage was forced to accept a humiliating peace that marked the end of its military and political power.

Rome imposed severe terms, including reducing the Carthaginian fleet to just ten ships and demanding a massive war indemnity.

Although Hannibal survived, he later went into exile and spent the rest of his life evading Roman agents.

The victory at Zama solidified Rome's position as the undisputed power in the western Mediterranean and laid the foundation for its expansion into other territories.

13

The Battle of Magnesia

The Battle of Magnesia occurred in 190 BC and was a decisive engagement that ended the Seleucid Empire's threat to Rome's interests in Asia Minor.

The battle took place on the plains near Magnesia ad Sipylum, in what is now Turkey.

The conflict arose from the expansionist ambitions of Antiochus III the Great, who, after consolidating his power in the East, turned his attention westward with the goal of extending his rule in Asia Minor, inevitably clashing with Rome's growing influence in the region.

Determined to protect their Greek allies and secure their dominance, the Romans dispatched an army under the command of Lucius Cornelius Scipio Asiaticus, supported by his brother, the renowned general Scipio Africanus, who had previously achieved victory at Zama against Hannibal.

The Roman army consisted of approximately 30,000 to 35,000 soldiers.

The infantry was composed of well-trained legions organized in maniples, providing significant flexibility in combat.

Greek and Asiatic allies also contributed auxiliary troops.

The Roman cavalry, though smaller in number than the infantry, was supported by allied horsemen, including the Thessalians, known for their skill and bravery.

Additionally, the Romans brought catapults and other siege engines to counter any unexpected fortifications.

On the other hand, Antiochus III's Seleucid army was considerably larger, numbering around 50,000 to 70,000 soldiers.

These included Macedonian-style heavy infantry phalanxes, formed in compact lines; mercenaries from various regions; light archers and slingers; and an impressive cavalry force, which featured cataphracts—heavily armored elite heavy cavalry.

The most striking element of Antiochus' army was his contingent of war elephants, numbering around 50 to 60, strategically positioned at the front to break enemy lines and cause panic.

Antiochus also deployed war chariots equipped with scythed wheels, designed to charge through and disrupt infantry formations.

The battle began at dawn, with the Seleucid forces arranged in an extensive formation: heavy infantry in the center, elephants interspersed along the line, and cavalry and chariots positioned on the flanks.

Antiochus personally commanded the cavalry on the right wing, confident in his ability to outflank and encircle the Romans.

Scipio Asiaticus, in turn, placed the legions at the center, supported by his Greek allies and auxiliaries on the flanks.

The Roman strategy relied on withstanding the initial impact and exploiting any weaknesses in the enemy flanks.

The battle began with an aggressive charge by the Seleucid war chariots, which swiftly advanced toward the Roman lines.

However, the Roman response was meticulously planned: the soldiers opened their ranks, allowing the chariots to pass through while attacking them with spears and javelins from the sides.

The chariots, unable to turn or maneuver effectively, were quickly neutralized, causing confusion within Antiochus' ranks.

Next, the war elephants advanced, but the Roman legions, trained to handle such threats, countered with volleys of javelins and the sound of trumpets, causing several elephants to panic and turn back, trampling through the Seleucid lines.

The ensuing disorder allowed the Roman infantry to advance in disciplined formation, striking at the Seleucid phalanx, which began to lose cohesion.

On the right flank, Antiochus personally led a charge with his heavy cavalry, initially achieving success by pushing back the Roman auxiliary troops.

However, the Roman cavalry, supported by the Thessalians, counterattacked and stabilized the situation.

On the left flank, the Seleucid cavalry failed to make significant progress, and the lack of coordination on this front further weakened Antiochus' position.

As the battle wore on, Antiochus' central phalanx found itself surrounded and increasingly disorganized.

The Romans, aware of their advantage, pressed forward aggressively, forcing the Seleucid soldiers to retreat and fragmenting their formation.

Antiochus' cavalry, unable to regroup and with its flanks exposed, scattered, leaving the infantry unprotected.

The result was a decisive defeat for Antiochus.

It is estimated that around 10,000 Seleucid soldiers were killed in the battle, while Roman casualties were much lower, approximately 2,000.

Antiochus withdrew from the field and soon accepted the peace terms imposed by Rome, which included relinquishing control over much of Asia Minor and paying a substantial financial indemnity.

The victory at Magnesia solidified Rome as the hegemonic power in the eastern Mediterranean and marked the decline of Seleucid power.

Rome's influence extended across Asia Minor, and the Republic's dominance was recognized throughout the region.

Although Antiochus survived, his empire was weakened and entered an irreversible phase of decline.

This battle was not only a turning point in Roman history but also redefined the balance of power in the Hellenistic world.

14

The Battle of Pydna

The Battle of Pydna took place in 168 BC and was the decisive confrontation between the Roman Republic and the Kingdom of Macedonia, led by King Perseus, during the Third Macedonian War.

This war arose after years of mounting tensions between Rome and Macedonia, as the expansion of Roman influence in the Hellenistic region had been a cause of concern for the Macedonians.

Rome, eager to solidify its dominance in the eastern Mediterranean, viewed King Perseus as a potential threat due to his alliance policies with other Greek powers and his refusal to submit to Roman demands.

The Roman army was commanded by Consul Lucius Aemilius Paullus, an experienced leader chosen for his military expertise and understanding of the geopolitical situation.

Under his command, the Roman legions numbered around 30,000 troops, comprising heavy infantry legionaries, auxiliary forces, light cavalry, and specialized units skilled in siege warfare and the use of war machines.

On the other hand, Perseus' Macedonian army consisted of approximately 40,000 men.

The backbone of his force was the famed Macedonian phalanx, a heavy infantry formation wielding long spears known as sarissas, whose length and tightly packed coordination had been the cornerstone of Macedonian military supremacy since the time of Philip II and Alexander the Great.

Alongside the phalanx, Perseus had a contingent of light infantry, archers, heavy cavalry, and Greek mercenaries hired to support the flanks and conduct rapid raids.

The terrain near Pydna, with its hills and a nearby river, offered mixed conditions that would test the capabilities of both armies.

The confrontation began in the early hours of the day, with both forces deployed in formation.

Aemilius Paullus ordered his legions to advance in a disciplined line, leaving space for maneuvering and adapting to the enemy's deployment.

The Macedonian phalanx, organized in compact ranks, moved in unison, presenting an almost impenetrable wall of spears.

In the initial clashes, the phalanx advanced, pushing back the Roman front lines and inflicting significant casualties due to the effectiveness of their sarissas.

However, the Macedonian formation, though formidable from the front, was less flexible on uneven terrain.

Aemilius Paullus, shrewdly exploiting the terrain, had the Romans strategically retreat toward areas with gentle slopes and inclines, which disrupted the cohesion of the phalanx.

At a critical moment, gaps began to appear in the Macedonian line as the formation struggled to maintain unity on uneven ground.

The Roman legions, well-trained for close combat, capitalized on these weaknesses.

The legionaries surged into the gaps with their gladius, attacking at close quarters and dismantling the Macedonian ranks from within.

The Roman cavalry also engaged, flanking the Macedonian cavalry units and disrupting any attempts by Perseus to reinforce his formation.

The Macedonian king, seeing his army collapse, tried to reorganize his forces and sent reinforcements from the rear, but chaos and panic had already gripped his troops.

The fighting raged on for hours, with the Macedonians desperately trying to hold their position, but Roman tactical superiority ultimately prevailed.

Macedonian casualties were devastating, with over 20,000 soldiers killed on the battlefield and thousands more captured.

The Roman legions, though they also suffered losses, secured a decisive victory with approximately 1,000 casualties.

Aemilius Paullus oversaw the surrender of the survivors and the capture of Perseus' senior officers.

The consequences of the Battle of Pydna were far-reaching.

With the Roman victory, Macedonia lost its status as an independent kingdom and was divided into four autonomous republics under Roman supervision.

Perseus was captured and brought to Rome, where he was paraded as a prisoner in Aemilius Paullus' triumph before being imprisoned.

This victory cemented Rome's power over Greece and the region, marking the end of Macedonian resistance and paving the way for full Roman domination in the eastern

Mediterranean.

The Macedonian phalanx, once the most feared military force in the ancient world, proved inferior to the adaptable and disciplined Roman legion on shifting terrain and under superior tactical leadership.

15

The Battle of Corinth

The Battle of Corinth took place in 146 BC and marked the culmination of tensions between the Roman Republic and the Achaean League, a federation of Greek city-states.

The Roman Republic, having consolidated its influence in the Mediterranean region, would not tolerate challenges to its hegemony.

The Achaean League, under the leadership of ambitious figures and fueled by growing dissatisfaction with Roman domination, saw an opportunity to assert its independence.

Roman Consul Lucius Mummius led the Roman army with the goal of crushing Greek resistance once and for all and establishing Rome's complete control over the Hellenic peninsula.

The Roman forces numbered approximately 30,000 men, including heavy infantry legions, well-equipped cavalry, and auxiliary troops.

These forces were supported by siege engines and light artillery capable of devastating walls and dispersing compact infantry formations.

Rome brought with it vast military experience and exceptional discipline, honed through campaigns across the Mediterranean.

The Achaean League, on the other hand, assembled an army of about 20,000 fighters.

Although their force was primarily composed of hoplite

infantry, equipped with spears and heavy shields, it also included a smaller number of peltasts, light infantry soldiers armed with javelins, and a limited cavalry contingent.

Despite their numerical and material disadvantage, the Achaean army was driven by a strong sense of defending their homeland and freedom.

The leadership of the Achaean League fell to Critolaus, a passionate leader but less experienced in large-scale battle tactics compared to his Roman counterpart.

The battle took place near the city of Corinth, a strategically significant stronghold and symbol of Greek pride.

The city was surrounded by hills that offered some defensive advantage, but the Romans, with their clear superiority in siege machinery and artillery, were able to turn these conditions to their advantage.

Mummius ordered a formation in three lines, with heavy infantry at the front, auxiliaries on the flanks, and cavalry positioned for flanking maneuvers.

The artillery, consisting of ballistae and catapults, was positioned at strategic points to bombard the Achaean positions and break their morale.

The engagement began with a massive bombardment by the Roman war machines, which inflicted significant damage on the Achaean hoplite lines.

The Greek formations, renowned for their resilience, struggled to maintain cohesion under the constant barrage of projectiles.

Despite this, Critolaus sought to maintain his troops' morale and ordered an advance of the phalanx, hoping to leverage the compact defensive structure of his soldiers.

However, the Romans were prepared.

After the artillery barrage had worn down the Achaeans, they launched their heavy infantry in a calculated frontal assault.

The legions advanced under the disciplined orders of their centurions, maintaining a formation that combined force and maneuverability.

When the Achaean forces attempted a counterattack to outflank the Romans, Mummius' cavalry charged in from the flanks, dismantling any maneuver attempts and sowing confusion in the Greek ranks.

The Achaean light infantry was unable to withstand the momentum of the legionaries and soon found themselves retreating toward the walls of Corinth.

The battle became chaotic as the Romans broke through the city's outer defenses, forcing the Achaeans into a desperate retreat.

Hand-to-hand combat in the streets of Corinth was brutal; the disciplined and efficient Romans overwhelmed the Greek defenders, who fought with the courage of those defending their homeland but lacked the necessary cohesion.

Achaean casualties were devastating, with over 15,000 soldiers killed or captured, and the remainder scattered.

The Romans, though they also suffered significant losses, with approximately 1,000 dead and wounded, managed to maintain their formation's integrity and secure victory.

Mummius ordered the city of Corinth to be sacked as punishment and a warning to any other Greek city-state contemplating rebellion against Rome.

The city, one of the richest and most culturally vibrant in

Greece, was burned, and its treasures and works of art were taken to Rome as spoils.

The consequences of the battle and the subsequent destruction of Corinth marked the end of organized Greek resistance and the beginning of absolute Roman domination over Greece.

The Achaean League was dissolved, and Greece was incorporated as a province of the Roman Republic, securing control that would last for centuries.

The victory at Corinth solidified Rome's reputation as an unstoppable force and sent a clear message to any Mediterranean power that might challenge its hegemony.

16

The Battle of Numantia

The Battle of Numantia took place in 133 BC and marked the climax of Celtiberian resistance against the expansion of the Roman Republic in the Iberian Peninsula.

Numantia, a city located in what is now the province of Soria, had withstood Roman attacks for over two decades.

Renowned for the bravery and determination of its defenders, it became a symbol of freedom and resistance against Roman might.

This final campaign was led by Publius Cornelius Scipio Aemilianus, the same general who had destroyed Carthage in the Third Punic War, chosen for his reputation as a relentless and methodical strategist.

The Roman army, under Scipio's command, numbered around 30,000 men, including well-trained heavy infantry legions, light infantry auxiliaries, cavalry, and siege engines such as catapults and ballistae.

The Romans also brought skilled engineers, enabling them to construct fortifications and implement effective siege tactics.

On the other side, Numantia had a much smaller force of around 8,000 fighters—men and women determined to defend their city to the death.

The Numantines were known for their fierce resistance, intimate knowledge of the terrain, and unwavering resolve, making them formidable opponents despite their numerical disadvantage.

Scipio opted for a strategy of attrition and encirclement rather than a frontal assault, understanding that Numantia's fortifications and the tenacity of its defenders made a direct attack too costly.

He ordered the construction of a 9-kilometer perimeter around the city, consisting of a defensive wall reinforced with watchtowers and ditches.

The Numantine garrison, though fierce, watched as their chances of receiving reinforcements or supplies dwindled as the Roman wall closed in around them.

With no possibility of external aid and their escape routes cut off, the city was completely isolated.

The battle developed into a prolonged siege and war of attrition.

Scipio instructed his troops to maintain constant pressure, launching occasional attacks to weaken the city's defenses and exhaust its inhabitants.

Catapults and ballistae fired flaming projectiles and heavy stones at the city's walls and buildings, causing destruction and undermining Numantine morale.

Despite the relentless pressure, the Celtiberians made several desperate sorties against the Roman lines, inflicting significant casualties on the besiegers but failing to break the siege.

These raids, while heroic, further depleted their numbers and drained their resources.

The scarcity of food and water began to take a heavy toll on Numantia.

The conditions became unbearable, and hunger and disease

began to decimate the population.

The Numantines continued to defend the city with unyielding determination, knowing that surrender was not an option.

The resistance lasted for months, but eventually, the situation became untenable.

The lack of food pushed the population to the brink of collapse, and desperation led some to consider extreme acts, including cannibalism.

When the final attempts to break the siege failed, the leaders of Numantia, realizing the city could hold out no longer, decided they would rather die than surrender.

Many families chose suicide, and the bravest warriors performed one last act of defiance by setting fire to the city and destroying what little remained to prevent it from falling into Roman hands.

The Romans eventually entered a city in ruins, finding a scene of utter devastation.

Few Numantines survived, and those who did were taken as prisoners and sold into slavery or brought to Rome to be paraded in Scipio's triumph.

Roman casualties were moderate, numbering only a few hundred, while the population of Numantia was nearly wiped out, leaving only a handful of survivors.

Rome's victory over Numantia marked not only the defeat of a city but the end of organized Celtiberian resistance in the Iberian Peninsula.

Scipio was honored in Rome for his success, and the fall of Numantia became a symbol of Rome's power and determination to crush any source of opposition, no matter how fierce or prolonged.

The story of Numantia became a legendary tale of resistance and sacrifice, serving as a reminder of the cost of defying the might of Rome.

17

The Battle of Aquae Sextiae

Fought in 102 BC, the Battle of Aquae Sextiae was a decisive engagement between the Roman Republic and the Germanic tribes of the Teutones and Ambrones, part of the Cimbrian Wars.

This battle marked a turning point in Rome's efforts to contain barbarian invasions that threatened to destabilize its northern frontiers.

Aquae Sextiae, modern-day Aix-en-Provence in southern France, served as the site of this brutal and strategically significant confrontation.

The Roman leader, Gaius Marius, an experienced consul and military reformer, was tasked with commanding Roman forces at a time when Rome's survival hung by a thread after a series of humiliating defeats at the hands of the Germanic tribes.

The Roman army under Marius numbered around 40,000 well-trained soldiers, organized into legions and supported by auxiliaries.

Marius' military reforms had strengthened the Roman legions, making them better equipped and more prepared to face unconventional enemies.

The Roman forces included heavy legionary infantry, light auxiliary cohorts, cavalry, and engineers capable of constructing defensive structures and traps.

The Teutones, along with their allies the Ambrones, formed a massive force of around 100,000 to 150,000 people, including women and children, as they traveled as a community in search of new lands.

These barbarian warriors, though less organized than the Roman legions, were renowned for their ferocity, physical strength, and determination.

Marius' plan centered on a strategy of divide and conquer.

Aware of the Teutones' customs and their tendency to move as an entire people, Marius used the terrain to his advantage.

He ordered his troops to fortify a camp on a hill, which lured the Teutones into a seemingly advantageous position that was, in fact, a trap.

Marius' camp was designed to withstand assaults, protected by ditches and palisades, limiting the effectiveness of a frontal attack by the Teutones.

The confrontation began with the Ambrones launching an initial assault, crossing a river to attack the Roman camp.

The Romans waited patiently until a significant portion of the Ambrone force had crossed the river.

At that moment, Marius ordered a surprise counterattack.

The legionaries, with their superior discipline and weaponry, engaged the disorganized Ambrones, who were unprepared for such a swift and coordinated response.

The fighting was fierce, with the Ambrones struggling to hold their positions as they were driven back toward the river.

The water ran red with the blood of the combatants, and the cries of the warriors mingled with the clash of swords and shields.

The Ambrones were almost completely annihilated, and those who managed to escape did so in disarray.

The Teutones, witnessing the defeat of their allies, launched an attack the following day, seeking to avenge the fallen and break the Roman encirclement.

However, Marius had stationed a hidden reserve force in the nearby hills, composed of legionaries and light auxiliaries.

As the Teutones charged the Roman camp, this reserve force attacked from the rear, throwing the barbarians into chaos and confusion.

Surrounded and assaulted from both flanks, the Teutones fought fiercely, but the discipline and tactical superiority of the Romans prevailed.

The battle turned into a massacre, with tens of thousands of Teutones killed or captured.

It is said that many chose suicide over surrender, with women killing their children and themselves to avoid enslavement.

Roman casualties were relatively low compared to the carnage suffered by the Teutones and Ambrones.

It is estimated that the Romans lost only a few thousand men, while the Germanic tribes saw nearly all their combatants killed or captured.

The victory at Aquae Sextiae secured Gaius Marius' prestige and boosted Rome's morale, which had been shaken by years of fear and uncertainty in the face of the barbarian threat.

The immediate consequence of the battle was the elimination of the Teutones as a threat, allowing Marius to focus his efforts on the upcoming campaign against the Cimbri, the other major Germanic invaders.

The victory cemented Marius' reputation as a savior of Rome and reaffirmed the effectiveness of his military reforms.

Moreover, the triumph at Aquae Sextiae bolstered confidence in the Roman legions and sent a clear message: Rome would not be easily subdued, even by numerous and formidable enemies.

The battle marked a milestone in Roman military history, showcasing the combination of strategy, discipline, and adaptability that would define Rome in the decades and centuries to come.

18

The Battle of Arausio

The Battle of Arausio occurred in 105 BC and stands as one of the most catastrophic defeats in the history of the Roman Republic.

It took place near the Rhône River in what is now southern France.

In this confrontation, the Romans faced the Cimbri and Teutones, migratory Germanic tribes seeking new lands to settle after being displaced by climatic changes and pressure from other tribes.

Tensions between these tribes and Rome had been escalating for years, particularly after earlier battles in which the Romans failed to halt their advance.

The Roman army consisted of approximately 80,000 infantry and 40,000 auxiliaries and non-combatants, totaling around 120,000 people.

Despite its imposing numbers, the Roman force was plagued by a lack of cohesion and coordination due to internal rivalries between its leaders, Consul Gnaeus Mallius Maximus and Proconsul Quintus Servilius Caepio.

The two commanders failed to cooperate, resulting in the division of their forces into two separate camps, which severely weakened the tactical effectiveness of the Roman army.

On the other hand, the Cimbri and their allies, including Teutonic contingents and other Germanic groups, assembled a force estimated at around 100,000 combatants.

These barbarian warriors were known for their great stature, physical strength, and ferocious combat abilities.

Although they lacked the organized military structure of the Romans, their mobility, determination, and knowledge of the terrain made them formidable opponents.

Led by their chiefs, notably Boiorix, the Cimbri were experts in ambushes and rapid movement tactics.

The battle unfolded chaotically from the start.

The rivalry between Maximus and Caepio prevented the unification of their forces, leaving the Romans in a vulnerable position.

Driven by distrust of Maximus and a desire for personal glory, Caepio decided to attack first without waiting for the arrival of Maximus' main army.

This hasty decision led to an uneven battle in which Caepio's troops were quickly overwhelmed by the ferocity of the Cimbri, who launched an enveloping attack that shattered the Roman lines.

Roman infantry, trapped between frontal charges and flanking enemy forces, was decimated in what became a massacre.

The Roman cavalry, though more mobile, was outmatched by the Cimbri's numerical superiority and flanking tactics, suffering heavy losses as well.

Maximus' army, which had held back in a rear position, was unable to organize an effective defense due to the panic and confusion caused by Caepio's defeat.

The Cimbri capitalized on the disorder to launch a second offensive, surrounding and crushing the remaining Roman forces.

Their use of the terrain and coordination of successive waves of attack allowed the Cimbri to close off all escape routes.

The fighting was fierce and lasted for hours, but Roman resistance eventually collapsed under the relentless pressure of the barbarians.

Roman casualties were colossal, with estimates ranging from 80,000 to 120,000 dead, including soldiers and non-combatants.

The Cimbri, on the other hand, suffered far fewer losses, solidifying their victory and delivering a devastating blow to Rome's prestige and morale.

The consequences of the Battle of Arausio were immense.

News of the defeat plunged Rome into panic, and the fear of a direct Germanic invasion became palpable.

Confidence in the Roman army's capabilities was shaken, and the Senate faced mounting pressure to reorganize and strengthen the legions.

This military disaster was one of the key factors that led to the military reforms of Gaius Marius, who implemented radical changes in the army's structure, training, and recruitment, preparing Rome for future confrontations and transforming it into a more formidable and efficient military force in the decades to come.

19

The Battle of Vercellae

Fought in 101 BC, it marked the final confrontation between the Roman Republic and the Cimbri, a Germanic tribe that had crossed the Alps in search of fertile lands to settle.

This conflict was the culmination of years of clashes between the Romans and northern tribes, which had seen Rome suffer crushing defeats, such as the Battle of Arausio in 105 BC, where the legions were annihilated.

However, Rome's response was swift.

Gaius Marius, a Roman general who had implemented significant reforms in the military, was appointed to lead the forces against the Cimbrian threat.

Marius' reforms included the professionalization of the army, intensive troop training, and the inclusion of soldiers from all social classes, which greatly improved the discipline and effectiveness of the legions.

The Roman army consisted of approximately 50,000 to 60,000 legionaries, including heavy infantry, auxiliary troops, and a well-equipped cavalry.

These forces were the result of a rigorous training process and a reorganization that ensured every legionary was prepared to execute complex battlefield maneuvers.

Gaius Marius, known for his intelligence and tactical skill, commanded the forces with the support of his colleague Quintus Lutatius Catulus, who also led a portion of the legions.

The Roman army was equipped with short swords (gladius), spears (pilum), large shields (scutum), and wore segmented armor.

Roman tactics included the testudo formation for defense and the use of flexible cohort formations to maneuver in combat.

On the other hand, the Cimbri, led by Boiorix, mobilized an estimated force of around 120,000 warriors, including men, women, and youths who participated in the battle directly or indirectly.

The tribe was known for their great stature and physical strength, which instilled fear in their adversaries.

Their weaponry included long swords, axes, and spears, and their formations were more fluid and less organized than those of the Romans.

However, their sheer numbers and ferocity partially compensated for this lack of structure.

The battle took place on the plains of Vercellae, in northern Italy.

Marius carefully selected the terrain to maximize the advantages of the Roman legions.

The open plain allowed the Romans to deploy their forces in a wide formation and fully utilize the discipline of their troops.

The Cimbri, confident from their previous victories, advanced on the Roman line with a formidable force, aiming to overwhelm the legionaries with their sheer weight and numbers.

Boiorix, leading his warriors from the front, ordered a mass advance—a tactic that had worked well in previous battles but underestimated Marius' ability to anticipate their movements.

The battle began with a brutal clash.

The Cimbri advanced with war cries, launching their first waves of warriors, but were met by a volley of pilum, which wreaked havoc on their ranks and disrupted their advance.

The legionaries, under the command of Marius and Catulus, held their positions and waited for the enemy to close in before responding with a coordinated charge.

The disciplined formation of the legions allowed the Romans to face the Cimbrian horde without breaking ranks.

The hand-to-hand combat was intense, with the Cimbri attacking with characteristic ferocity and the Romans responding with meticulous training and precise tactical maneuvers.

Marius implemented an envelopment strategy, ordering the Roman cavalry to flank the enemy and attack from the sides.

This maneuver split the Cimbrian forces and forced them to fight on multiple fronts, reducing their effectiveness.

As the battle progressed, the relentless pressure from the legions and the continuous assaults on the flanks caused the Cimbrian formation to begin fragmenting.

The situation became critical for the Cimbri when Boiorix and several of their leaders were killed in combat, plunging the tribe into chaos and despair.

The casualties were devastating for the Cimbri.

It is estimated that over 100,000 of their warriors and followers were killed on the battlefield, and a large number were captured.

Roman losses, though significant, were considerably lower

thanks to Marius' preparation and tactics.

The victory at Vercellae ended the Cimbrian threat and cemented Marius as one of the greatest heroes of the Roman Republic.

The battle had far-reaching consequences: it secured Rome's northern frontier and demonstrated the effectiveness of Marius' military reforms, which laid the foundation for Rome's future military dominance.

Marius' reputation as the savior of Rome was solidified, and his success boosted his political influence, though it also set the stage for internal rivalries that would eventually lead to civil conflict within the Republic.

20

The Battle of the Sabis River

Also known as the Battle Against the Nervii, it was fought in 57 BC as part of Julius Caesar's campaign in Gaul.

After consolidating his control over the northern and central Gallic tribes, Caesar turned his attention to the warlike Belgic tribes, renowned for their ferocity in battle and fierce independence.

The Nervii, one of the most powerful and proud tribes in the region, along with other Belgic tribes like the Atrebates and Viromandui, decided to resist the Roman advance.

Aware of their reputation and military strength, Caesar prepared for what would become one of the most challenging and bloody battles of his campaign.

Caesar's army consisted of about eight legions, totaling approximately 30,000 to 40,000 soldiers, along with auxiliaries, cavalry, and light artillery.

Each legion was made up of disciplined heavy infantry, equipped with pilum (javelins), gladius (short swords), and rectangular shields (scutum).

Caesar, personally leading the army, was supported by trusted officers such as Titus Labienus and Quintus Titurius Sabinus.

The troops were organized into fortified camps, which the Romans meticulously built before any engagement.

Opposite them, the Nervii and their allies fielded an estimated force of around 60,000 to 75,000 warriors.

Although the Belgic tribes lacked the Roman military organization, they made up for it with their bravery and ferocity on the battlefield.

The Nervii, in particular, were known for avoiding the use of chariots and cavalry, relying instead on their heavy infantry and ambush tactics.

The tribal leaders, commanding through collective leadership, had chosen terrain they knew well, near the Sabis River (likely the modern-day Selle River in northern France), to maximize their advantage and minimize Rome's tactical superiority.

The battle began as Caesar and his legions advanced to establish a camp on the river's bank.

While the Romans were busy constructing fortifications, the Nervii launched a surprise attack, using the cover of dense forests and their intimate knowledge of the terrain.

The speed and violence of the assault caught the Roman legions off guard.

Nervii warriors crossed the river in force and charged with overwhelming momentum, breaking through the initial Roman formations and causing chaos among the legionaries.

Seeing the imminent danger, Caesar ordered his centurions to quickly organize their men into combat formation.

His officers moved swiftly to coordinate the cohorts and face the onslaught.

The situation for the Romans became critical at several points.

The legions, scattered and without time to properly organize, fought tenaciously, but the Nervii, driven by their determination to defend their land, broke through the Roman defensive lines in multiple parts of the battlefield.

The pressure was so intense that Caesar himself was forced to draw his sword and join the fight directly, encouraging his men and showing them that victory was still within reach.

Labienus, commanding one of the legions on a nearby hill, understood the gravity of the situation and, without waiting for orders, led a decisive counterattack from his elevated position.

This maneuver allowed the legions to fall back and regroup into a more cohesive formation.

The Romans began to regain control of the battle, pushing the Nervii back toward the river.

The use of the pilum proved devastating, as the javelins pierced through enemy lines and sowed confusion among the Nervii warriors.

Despite the legions' advance, the Nervii did not retreat easily and fought to the last breath, displaying a bravery that even the Romans admired.

It is said that the majority of the Nervii warriors perished on the battlefield, leaving the ground covered with bodies.

Roman losses were also significant; some cohorts lost more than half their men, but Caesar's discipline and tactics ultimately prevailed.

The victory at the Sabis River secured Caesar's control over the region and significantly weakened Belgic resistance.

However, the consequences of the battle were devastating for the Nervii, who were nearly annihilated as a military force.

In his Commentaries on the Gallic War, Caesar

acknowledged the bravery of the Nervii, making it clear that although his victory was decisive, the battle demonstrated the ferocity and defiance the Romans faced in their expansion through Gaul.

Caesar's reputation as a capable and daring commander was further solidified, and this victory helped strengthen his political position in Rome, paving the way for his future conquests and eventual rise to power.

21

The Battle of Carrhae

Fought in 53 BC, it was a decisive confrontation between the Roman Republic and the Parthian Empire, two powers clashing in a theater of operations driven by political ambition and territorial greed.

Marcus Licinius Crassus, a member of the First Triumvirate alongside Julius Caesar and Pompey, was one of the wealthiest and most powerful men in Rome, but his ambition knew no bounds.

Eager to achieve military glory to rival that of his peers, Crassus launched a campaign to conquer Parthia, a kingdom renowned for its vast resources and lethal cavalry.

Crasus commanded an army comprising about seven legions, totaling approximately 35,000 to 40,000 legionaries, supplemented by around 4,000 cavalry and 4,000 light auxiliaries.

While experienced in civil war and campaigns in the Italian Peninsula, Crassus had no experience fighting an enemy like the Parthians, whose warfare tactics relied on extreme mobility and masterful use of cavalry and mounted archers.

The Parthians, under the command of their general Surena, deployed a smaller force of 10,000 to 12,000 horse archers and an elite unit of cataphracts, heavily armored cavalry.

The strategic context was challenging for Crassus.

Despite the advice of his allies and subordinates, Crassus chose to march through the vast and arid plains of Mesopotamia, ignoring safer or more strategic routes that would have provided better defensive positions.

Meanwhile, Surena, a young and cunning commander, used the terrain to his advantage.

He concealed his forces in the desert and maneuvered them in such a way that Crassus could neither anticipate their presence nor predict their movements.

The battle unfolded when Crassus and his legions arrived on the plains of Carrhae, where the Parthians suddenly appeared, arrayed in an impressive but numerically limited formation, at least to the Romans' eyes.

Overconfident and underestimating his enemy, Crassus ordered his troops to form a compact square, a strategy designed to withstand direct attacks but one that would prove a fatal mistake.

The Parthian horse archers began their assault, unleashing a relentless rain of arrows upon the Romans.

Parthian arrows, known for their extreme effectiveness and fired from powerful composite bows, inflicted heavy casualties even from long distances.

The legionaries, unable to counterattack effectively due to the distance and their inadequate cavalry support, began to fall into disarray.

The Parthian strategy relied on the tactical use of the "carousel" or shoot-and-retreat tactic.

The mounted archers would ride close enough to unleash a deadly volley of arrows, then retreat before the Romans could respond.

Crassus attempted to deploy his cavalry, led by his son, Publius Licinius Crassus, to break the enemy line and pursue the skirmishers.

However, Publius and his force, consisting of around 1,300 cavalrymen and several auxiliary cohorts, were quickly surrounded by the heavy cavalry of the cataphracts and archers, becoming trapped in a deadly ring.

In a display of courage, Publius fought to the end, and seeing the imminent defeat, he committed suicide alongside his officers to avoid capture.

With the loss of his son and a significant portion of his forces, Crassus and the remaining soldiers were left demoralized and weakened.

Surena's strategy continued, exhausting the Romans with relentless waves of arrows while the cataphracts maintained pressure without engaging in a full frontal charge.

As the day wore on, the heat and lack of water took a severe toll on the Roman legionaries, who found themselves increasingly surrounded and with no options for escape.

The battle concluded with the annihilation of most of the Roman army.

It is estimated that at least 20,000 legionaries were killed, another 10,000 were captured, and the rest fled back to Carrhae.

Crassus, attempting to negotiate his surrender, was betrayed and killed.

According to tradition, the Parthians, in a symbolic gesture representing Crassus' greed, poured molten gold down his throat.

The consequences of the Battle of Carrhae were devastating for Rome.

Not only was an entire army and a consul lost, but Rome's reputation for invincibility was also severely damaged.

This defeat marked a shift in Rome's eastern policy and highlighted the power and sophistication of the Parthian Empire.

The confrontation left a scar on the Roman psyche and served as a reminder of the dangers of unchecked ambition and underestimating the enemy.

Furthermore, Crassus' death destabilized the Triumvirate, accelerating the rivalry between Julius Caesar and Pompey, which would eventually lead to another civil war in Rome.

22

The Battle of Alesia

Fought in 52 BC, it marked the climax of the Gallic Wars, a series of campaigns in which Julius Caesar, governor of Transalpine Gaul, sought to consolidate Roman control over the region and bolster his prestige in Rome.

Alesia, a formidable fortified city in the territory of the Arverni, served as the stronghold of the Gallic leader Vercingetorix, a warrior and strategist who had managed to unite multiple Gallic tribes under his command.

This rare cohesion among the Gallic tribes posed a serious threat to Roman hegemony, which had until then maintained dominance over Gaul through a combination of diplomacy, alliances, and military force.

Caesar's forces consisted of approximately 50,000 Roman legionaries, seasoned veterans who had fought for years in the region.

These soldiers belonged to legions such as the renowned Legio X Equestris, known for its loyalty and combat prowess.

Caesar also had around 10,000 auxiliaries, including archers, slingers, and a contingent of Germanic cavalry recruited to counter the superior Gallic cavalry.

The legions were led by trusted officers like Titus Labienus and Gaius Trebonius, who commanded strategic divisions of the Roman forces.

Facing him, Vercingetorix commanded a force of between 80,000 and 100,000 warriors inside Alesia, along with approximately 240,000 reinforcements from various Gallic tribes advancing to break the siege.

The Gallic cavalry was superior in number and well-trained, posing a significant threat to the Roman lines.

The terrain around Alesia was particularly challenging.

The city was situated on an elevated plateau surrounded by rivers and hills, making it naturally defensive.

Aware of the difficulties of a direct assault, Caesar opted for a bold and methodical plan: to besiege the city and deprive it of supplies.

To achieve this, he ordered the construction of an impressive feat of military engineering: a siege line approximately 15 kilometers long encircling the city, consisting of palisades, double ditches filled with water, traps, and watchtowers.

To protect against the approaching Gallic relief army, he also commanded the construction of a second line of fortifications, creating a double circumvallation that allowed the Romans to defend against both the city's defenders and external attackers.

The siege began with the isolation of Alesia.

Vercingetorix, understanding the gravity of the situation, sent his cavalry to attempt to break through the siege and seek help.

The Gallic horsemen successfully evaded the Roman defenses and summoned allied tribes to come to their aid.

Meanwhile, inside Alesia, the situation became dire; food supplies were rapidly depleting, and conditions worsened.

In an act of desperation, Vercingetorix ordered the non-combatants expelled from the city to conserve resources.

However, Caesar refused to open his lines, leaving the civilians trapped between the city and the Roman fortifications, where they suffered from hunger and cold.

When the relief army arrived, it consisted of a heterogeneous mass of tribes with varying tactics and leadership.

The assault began with coordinated attacks from outside the walls of Alesia and from within the city.

The allied Gallic cavalry attempted to flank and breach the Roman fortifications, but Caesar's Germanic cavalry allies, known for their brutality and skill, held them back in fierce skirmishes.

Wave after wave of assaults continued for days; Roman defenses were pressured at various points, forcing Caesar to shift his reserves from one part of the perimeter to another, ensuring that the lines did not break.

The fighting was intense, with Gallic horsemen charging against wooden stakes and legionaries holding their ground with pilum and gladius in hand.

The most critical moment came when a section of the outer fortifications began to give way under the pressure of a massive assault led by a combined force of Gallic warriors.

Recognizing the need for visible and decisive leadership, Caesar placed himself at the head of a reinforcing charge.

Clad in his scarlet cloak, the symbol of supreme command, Caesar led his men in a counteroffensive that inspired his troops to stand firm and fight back.

With the support of his trusted commanders, the Romans closed the breach and repelled the attackers, inflicting heavy casualties on the Gallic forces.

The relief army, after days of futile assaults and exhausted by their lack of organization and coordination, began to lose morale.

The tribes started to retreat in disarray, leaving the defenders of Alesia with no hope of rescue.

Vercingetorix, knowing that continued resistance would doom his people, called a council and made the decision to surrender.

In a moment that would be etched into history, he mounted his horse and rode out of the city to present himself to Caesar, throwing his weapons at Caesar's feet as a gesture of submission.

The consequences of the Battle of Alesia were monumental.

Caesar's victory solidified Roman control over Gaul and elevated his political status in Rome, where he was celebrated as a hero.

However, this triumph also planted the seeds of civil war, as Caesar's growing popularity and power aroused suspicion and fear within the Senate and among his political rivals.

For the Gauls, the surrender of Vercingetorix symbolized the end of organized resistance and the loss of their autonomy, marking the beginning of the region's Romanization.

23

The Battle of Pharsalus

Fought on August 9, 48 B.C., was the turning point in the civil war between Julius Caesar and Pompey the Great.

This conflict arose following the collapse of the political alliance known as the First Triumvirate, which included Caesar, Pompey, and Crassus.

After Crassus's death at the Battle of Carrhae and the growing rivalry between Caesar and Pompey, the Roman Senate, heavily influenced by Pompey, ordered Caesar to disband his legions and return to Rome.

Refusing to relinquish his power, Caesar crossed the Rubicon in 49 B.C., igniting a civil war.

After a series of campaigns and minor skirmishes, Pompey and his senatorial allies retreated to Greece, where they aimed to regroup and launch a decisive counteroffensive against Caesar.

Pompey's army at Pharsalus was formidable: approximately 45,000 men, including 7,000 cavalry.

The heavy infantry consisted mainly of veteran legionaries, many of whom had survived previous campaigns, granting them an advantage in experience and morale.

Pompey, a seasoned commander with victories in Asia Minor and the wars against pirates, was confident in his abilities and the strength of his cavalry.

The exiled senators and other Roman nobles were also present, adding an air of prestige and political pressure.

Caesar, on the other hand, commanded a smaller force of around 22,000 legionaries and approximately 1,000 cavalry.

However, his men were fiercely loyal, battle-hardened soldiers known for their iron discipline and ability to adapt swiftly on the battlefield.

Caesar led with charisma and remarkable tactical skill, relying on the loyalty of his troops and his keen understanding of the enemy's weaknesses.

The battlefield chosen by Pompey at Pharsalus, an open plain near the Enipeus River, was intended to capitalize on his superiority in cavalry.

Pompey's strategy was to use his cavalry, commanded by Titus Labienus, to flank Caesar's forces and disrupt their lines.

Meanwhile, his infantry would hold their ground and wear down Caesar's legionaries until the cavalry could envelop and crush the enemy.

Caesar, however, understanding his opponent's plan, devised a clever strategy to neutralize Pompey's advantage.

He ordered six cohorts to remain hidden at an oblique angle behind his own cavalry, prepared to act as a barrier against the anticipated flanking maneuver.

The day of the battle dawned under a scorching sun.

The armies lined up, with Caesar positioning his legionaries in the classic three-line formation and placing his cavalry on the right flank.

Pompey, confident in his plan, ordered his troops to hold their positions, forcing Caesar to advance.

This advance was a risky maneuver for Caesar's troops,

who had to cover a considerable distance before engaging, potentially exhausting their energy.

Despite this, Caesar's legionaries maintained their discipline and advanced in terrifying silence, finally clashing with Pompey's lines.

The decisive moment came when Pompey's cavalry charged from the left flank, aiming to envelop Caesar's men.

It was then that Caesar deployed his reserve of six cohorts, which emerged from their hidden position and struck the Pompeian cavalry with spears and coordinated movements.

The surprise and precision of the maneuver threw Pompey's cavalry into panic, causing them to retreat in disarray.

Seeing the disorganization of the enemy cavalry, Caesar's infantry intensified their attack, pushing forward with renewed momentum.

Pompey, witnessing his strategy collapse, panicked and ordered a general retreat.

However, the retreat quickly turned into a rout, and Caesar's forces seized the opportunity to launch a full offensive.

The casualties on Pompey's side were devastating: it is estimated that over 15,000 men were killed and another 24,000 captured.

Caesar's losses were significantly lower, around 1,200 men, thanks to his innovative tactics and the superior morale of his troops.

The defeat at Pharsalus marked the end of Pompey's power.

He fled to Egypt, where he was betrayed and assassinated on the orders of the young Pharaoh Ptolemy XIII, who sought to win Caesar's favor.

However, Pompey's death did not bring immediate stability.

When Caesar arrived in Egypt, he became embroiled in a complex internal conflict that ultimately led to his alliance with Cleopatra and the consolidation of his power.

The victory at Pharsalus established Caesar as the undisputed leader of Rome, though it paved the way for his eventual dictatorship and the tensions that would lead to his assassination in 44 B.C.

For Rome, the end of the civil war marked the transition from a republic to a more autocratic regime, laying the groundwork for the rise of the Empire under Augustus.

24

The Battle of Thapsus

Fought in 46 B.C., marked one of the final phases of the Roman civil war between Julius Caesar and the Pompeian faction.

After Pompey's death in Egypt, his remaining supporters sought to regroup in Africa, a strategic region that provided resources and the support of local allies, such as King Juba I of Numidia.

Under the leadership of Metellus Scipio and Cato the Younger, the Pompeians consolidated a powerful army that included veterans from previous campaigns and African contingents provided by Juba.

For Caesar, this final uprising in Africa posed a significant threat to his consolidation of power following his victories at Pharsalus and other regions.

The Pompeian army consisted of approximately 70,000 men, with around 40,000 experienced legionaries.

This force was bolstered by a sizable cavalry and a significant contingent of war elephants, numbering about 60, supplied by Juba I.

Caesar's forces, though smaller, benefited from the loyalty and experience of his troops.

He commanded roughly 40,000 men, divided among several legions, including veterans from his campaigns in Gaul and the recent civil wars.

These forces were renowned for their discipline and combat

skills.

Caesar's cavalry was numerically inferior but compensated with agility and maneuverability.

Caesar maintained unquestioned command over his troops and relied on key subordinates such as Mark Antony and Gaius Trebonius.

The battle took place near the city of Thapsus, in present-day Tunisia, on terrain that favored both defenders and attackers due to its open plains.

Caesar deployed his legions in a broad front, dividing his forces into two wings and positioning cavalry and his own war elephants on the flanks to prevent Pompeian cavalry from outflanking them.

Juba I's elephants were strategically placed on the wings of the Pompeian formation, a tactic aimed at sowing chaos among Caesar's lines and breaking the cohesion of his legionaries.

Caesar initiated the battle with a methodical offensive, advancing his legions in tight formation and ordering his archers and slingers to harass the war elephants.

The Pompeian response was fierce: their cavalry, led by Labienus, attempted a flanking maneuver, while the elephants charged forward with a deafening roar, aiming to crush Caesar's frontline troops.

However, Caesar had anticipated this tactic and instructed his men to target the elephants' legs and focus their spears on the mahouts, the elephant drivers.

The Caesarian resistance was highly effective; the wounded and uncontrollable elephants turned back against their own Pompeian lines, causing chaos and disarray.

The advance of Caesar's legions was relentless.

The Pompeian flanks began to collapse under the pressure of coordinated attacks and the skill of Caesar's legionaries.

Metellus Scipio's troops, though brave, could not withstand the disciplined push of Caesar's formations.

The defenders, driven by panic, began to retreat in disarray, while Cato the Younger and other leaders vainly tried to reorganize the resistance.

The Pompeian losses were severe: it is estimated that over 10,000 men died on the battlefield, with many others captured or scattered.

In contrast, Caesar's forces suffered minimal losses, a testament to his superior strategy and the effectiveness of his veteran soldiers.

Metellus Scipio managed to escape temporarily, only to meet his end shortly afterward while attempting to flee by sea.

Cato the Younger, seeing the imminent defeat and the end of the Republican cause, chose to commit suicide in Utica, an act that symbolized the steadfastness and determination of the old Roman elite in the face of tyranny.

The victory at Thapsus solidified Caesar's power in Rome, eliminating the last remnants of organized Pompeian resistance.

With the fall of the Republican leaders, Caesar emerged as dictator, holding near-absolute control over Rome.

This triumph paved the way for his political and administrative reforms, though it also sowed the seeds of the conspiracy that would lead to his assassination in 44 B.C.

25

The Battle of Munda

fought in 45 B.C., marked the final and decisive confrontation of the Roman civil war between Julius Caesar and the remnants of the Pompeian forces.

After Pompey's defeat at Pharsalus and his subsequent death in Egypt, the supporters of the republican cause did not disband.

Pompey's sons, Gnaeus and Sextus, along with the general Titus Labienus, managed to reorganize a formidable army in Hispania Ulterior, a region still sympathetic to the republican cause and a significant threat to Caesar's consolidation of power.

This region, rich in resources and strategically vital, became the last stronghold of resistance for the Pompeians.

The Pompeian army numbered approximately 70,000 men, including around 40,000 veteran legionaries and the rest made up of auxiliaries recruited from local tribes and Hispanic allies.

They also commanded a cavalry force of about 6,000 riders and several war machines, such as ballistae and scorpions, which were strategically positioned to reinforce their defenses.

Titus Labienus, an experienced strategist who had been one of Caesar's key lieutenants during the Gallic campaigns, provided crucial military leadership.

Gnaeus Pompey, though less experienced than his father, demonstrated determination and a willingness to fight to the end.

On his part, Caesar commanded an army of approximately 40,000 legionaries, many of whom were battle-hardened veterans from the Gallic campaigns and previous civil conflicts.

These men, though outnumbered by the Pompeians, had the advantage of unwavering loyalty to their leader and superior combat experience.

Caesar also had a cavalry force of about 8,000 riders and light auxiliaries specialized in skirmishes and rapid maneuvers.

Despite the numerical disadvantage, the morale of Caesar's forces was high, driven by the determination to end the civil war with a decisive victory.

The battle took place on the plains of Munda, in the southern Iberian Peninsula.

The terrain favored the defenders, with hills that the Pompeians used to position their forces and secure a strategic advantage.

Aware of the challenges posed by attacking an elevated position, Caesar opted for an aggressive and risky strategy.

He ordered his legions to deploy across a wide front, with the cavalry divided on both flanks to attempt an envelopment of the enemy.

The key to his plan was to demoralize and divide the Pompeians before they could fully exploit their numerical superiority.

The battle commenced with a methodical advance of Caesar's legions under constant fire from the Pompeian scorpions and ballistae.

The front lines of Caesar's forces endured the attack with discipline, while the archers and slingers returned fire, aiming to disrupt the enemy positions.

Caesar's cavalry, led by Gaius Trebonius and Lucius Cornelius Balbus, attempted several flank incursions but faced fierce resistance from Labienus's cavalry, who fought with skill and determination.

The turning point came when Caesar, seeing the lack of progress and the looming risk of a disastrous retreat, chose to expose himself at the front of his troops to inspire courage.

His presence on the front line, sword in hand and bearing his general's insignia, rallied his legionaries to intensify their efforts.

This heroic act spurred a renewed frontal assault by Caesar's legions, which, despite heavy losses, began to push uphill.

The hand-to-hand combat was brutal.

Legionaries from both sides exchanged blows for hours, with the ground soaked in blood.

Labienus, recognizing the danger posed by Caesar's renewed offensive, attempted to reinforce the Pompeian center, but his maneuver came too late.

Caesar's cavalry, now supported by light infantry, managed to break through the Pompeian right flank, unleashing chaos and disorganization among the enemy ranks.

Titus Labienus fell amidst the battle, further demoralizing Cnaeus Pompey's troops.

The Pompeians began to retreat in disarray, many of them slaughtered by Caesar's relentless cavalry as they pursued without mercy.

The Pompeian casualties exceeded 30,000 dead, with an undetermined number of prisoners, while Caesar's losses, though significant, were comparatively lower, totaling around 1,000 dead and several wounded.

The victory at Munda established Caesar as the undisputed master of Rome, effectively ending the civil war and leaving the Pompeian faction leaderless.

The consequences of the battle were profound.

With the death of Labienus and the capture and subsequent execution of Gnaeus Pompey shortly thereafter, the organized opposition to Caesar crumbled.

Under his command, Rome embarked on a process of political and administrative reforms that would alter the course of its history.

However, the concentration of power in Caesar's hands also sparked fear and resentment among certain factions of the Roman elite, paving the way for his assassination on the Ides of March in 44 B.C., just one year after his final great victory at Munda.

26

The Battle of Philippi

Fought in 42 B.C., was the decisive confrontation between the forces of the Second Triumvirate, led by Octavian (the future Augustus) and Mark Antony, and the Republican forces commanded by Marcus Junius Brutus and Gaius Cassius Longinus, the principal conspirators in the assassination of Julius Caesar on the Ides of March in 44 B.C.

Following Caesar's murder, Rome descended into political and military chaos.

The Senate, divided between supporters of the assassins and Caesar's loyalists, attempted to maintain a fragile balance, but a power struggle was inevitable.

Octavian, Mark Antony, and Lepidus formed the Second Triumvirate with the goal of consolidating control over Rome and avenging Caesar's death.

The forces of the Second Triumvirate, numbering approximately 100,000 men, included Caesar's veteran legions as well as others recruited by Octavian and Antony.

Octavian's troops, while numerous, included less experienced recruits due to the strain of recruitment following previous civil wars, whereas Antony's forces were formidable, led by a seasoned and capable battlefield commander.

Mark Antony played a pivotal role in planning and executing the military strategies, leveraging his boldness and extensive military expertise.

The Triumvirate's cavalry, numbering around 13,000 horsemen, provided significant maneuverability, and their resources included catapults and other siege engines to target enemy positions.

On the other side, the Republican forces of Brutus and Cassius fielded approximately 80,000 troops, most of them veterans who had previously fought under Pompey and other Republican leaders.

Both commanders, despite their experience, faced the immense pressure of leading their troops in a battle that could determine the survival of the Republic.

Morale in the Republican camp was high, driven by the conviction that they were fighting for Rome's freedom against the growing autocratic power of the triumvirs.

The Republicans also had a capable cavalry force, numbering around 8,000 horsemen, and had fortified their positions near Philippi, constructing palisades and trenches to protect their defenses.

The battlefield at Philippi, in Macedonia, was an open area with hills and a series of marshes that complicated troop movements.

Brutus and Cassius fortified their positions on two hills, separated by a wide plain.

Mark Antony, demonstrating his exceptional tactical skill, sought opportunities to divide the enemy forces and breach their defenses.

Octavian, who was ill during the campaign, played a more limited role in direct action, delegating command of his legions to trusted officers.

The battle began with a series of skirmishes and maneuvers.

Mark Antony launched a determined assault on the hill where Cassius was positioned, using siege engines to weaken the Republican defenses and force them to retreat.

Brutal hand-to-hand combat ensued, with Roman legionaries clashing against former comrades-in-arms.

Antony's advantage became evident as he successfully flanked Cassius's position, forcing him to retreat in disarray deeper into his lines.

At the same time, Brutus, capitalizing on the inexperience of Octavian's troops, launched a frontal assault, achieving a temporary victory by capturing Octavian's camp.

However, Brutus's success was not enough to offset Cassius's defeat.

Believing the entire battle was lost, Cassius, witnessing his positions overrun and his forces decimated, took his own life to avoid capture.

This act of despair deprived the Republicans of a key leader at a critical moment.

Upon learning of Cassius's death, Brutus reorganized his forces and tried to maintain a strong defensive position, hoping that the victory over Octavian's flank could be consolidated.

The second phase of the battle unfolded several days later, as both sides repositioned and regrouped their forces.

Antony, seeking to capitalize on the confusion in the enemy camp, launched a coordinated attack with Octavian, who, despite his illness, demonstrated determination by directing his troops from his litter.

The numerical superiority and renewed morale of the

Triumvirs gradually overwhelmed the Republican defenders.

Brutus's infantry, though fighting with courage and discipline, began to lose ground under the combined pressure of enemy forces and Antony's cavalry raids.

Seeing his army crumble under the weight of the attack, Brutus attempted an orderly retreat but soon realized that defeat was inevitable.

Unwilling to be captured and humiliated in Rome, he followed Cassius's example and took his own life on the battlefield, sealing the fate of the Republican forces.

Most of the surviving soldiers were either captured or scattered.

The consequences of the Battle of Philippi were profound.

The victory consolidated the power of the Second Triumvirate and eliminated the last major Republican threat.

Mark Antony and Octavian divided the Roman territories between them, with Antony taking control of the eastern provinces and Octavian securing the West.

This triumph accelerated Rome's transformation from a republic to an empire, culminating in the autocratic rule of Octavian, who would later become the first emperor, Augustus.

The end of Republican resistance marked the beginning of a new era in Roman history, characterized by the centralization of power in the hands of a single leader and the expansion of the empire toward its greatest glories and challenges.

27

The Battle of Actium

Fought on September 2, 31 B.C., was the decisive clash in the struggle for power during the late Roman Republic, pitting Octavian, the future Emperor Augustus, against Mark Antony and Cleopatra VII of Egypt.

This naval battle became a turning point, marking the end of the Roman Republic and the beginning of the Empire under Octavian's rule.

After years of tension and unstable political alliances, the relationship between Octavian and Mark Antony irreparably fractured when Antony formed a close alliance with Cleopatra, queen of Egypt.

This alliance raised suspicions and accusations of treason among the Romans.

The Senate, swayed by Octavian, declared war against Cleopatra, portraying her as the embodiment of an Eastern threat and thereby legitimizing the conflict.

Octavian's forces comprised a formidable fleet of approximately 400 ships, mainly triremes and quinqueremes, commanded by his ally and admiral Agrippa, a brilliant naval strategist.

These ships were fast and highly maneuverable, ideal for executing swift tactical maneuvers in open waters.

On land, Octavian commanded an army of around 80,000 infantry, many of whom were veterans of the civil wars, disciplined and motivated by the promise of a decisive victory.

Agrippa, an experienced commander, played a crucial role not only in planning the battle but also in executing the strategy of blockade and naval harassment that preceded the main engagement.

On the opposing side, Mark Antony and Cleopatra assembled a fleet of around 500 ships, including massive Egyptian warships known as deceremes, which dwarfed Octavian's vessels.

Although these ships were imposing and capable of carrying large contingents of soldiers and archers, their size made them slow and difficult to maneuver—a significant disadvantage compared to Octavian's agile ships.

Antony's land forces comprised about 60,000 soldiers, who, while well-trained, faced wavering morale due to the mix of Roman and Egyptian troops.

Cleopatra, aboard her flagship, contributed not only financial resources but also a symbolic and motivational presence, representing the strategic and personal alliance with Antony.

The battle unfolded in the waters of the Ambracian Gulf, off the coast of Actium in western Greece.

Octavian and Agrippa had effectively blockaded Antony's supply routes, weakening his ability to sustain a prolonged campaign.

Forced to confront Octavian, Antony's strategy aimed to break through and escape to open sea, where he hoped to regroup and fortify his position in Egypt.

However, Agrippa had meticulously arranged his forces to exploit the wind and the superior maneuverability of his ships.

Octavian's ships formed a tight and compact line, designed to withstand ramming attacks and exploit any gaps in the enemy's formation.

The battle began with Antony's ships advancing slowly, launching volleys of arrows and fire projectiles to break Octavian's line.

The heavier Egyptian ships attempted to ram Agrippa's triremes, but Octavian's lighter vessels skillfully evaded and struck the vulnerable flanks of the enemy ships, targeting their joints.

The fighting intensified in the center as Agrippa ordered a coordinated assault to push Antony's ships away from the coast, cutting off any chance of a land retreat.

The battle descended into chaos when Cleopatra's fleet, seeing the impending defeat, suddenly retreated, with her flagship leading the way to open sea.

Antony, caught off guard by Cleopatra's abrupt maneuver, decided to follow her, abandoning much of his fleet and army.

This move demoralized the remaining forces, who were swiftly overwhelmed by Octavian's ships.

Agrippa and his men capitalized on the confusion, encircling and capturing dozens of vessels, while others were set ablaze and sunk.

Antony suffered heavy losses, with over 200 ships destroyed and thousands of men killed or captured.

Most of his soldiers on land, seeing their leader's desperate situation and lacking naval support, surrendered or deserted.

Octavian's forces, on the other hand, suffered minimal casualties thanks to the effectiveness of their strategy and the leadership of Agrippa, who had proven to be a shrewd and calculating commander.

The consequences of the Battle of Actium were profound and transformative.

Antony and Cleopatra managed to escape to Alexandria, but their power and prestige were irreparably damaged.

A year later, both committed suicide as Octavian advanced on Egypt.

This victory established Octavian as the sole and supreme ruler of Rome.

In 27 B.C., Octavian proclaimed himself the first Roman emperor under the title Augustus, marking the end of the Republic and the beginning of the Roman Empire, which would expand and thrive for centuries to come.

28

The Battle of Teutoburg Forest

Fought in 9 A.D., was a pivotal conflict that marked the limit of Roman expansion into Germania and a turning point in Rome's military history.

This clash occurred amidst rising tensions between the Roman Empire and the Germanic tribes, who, though seemingly subdued under Roman rule, harbored deep resentment and a yearning for freedom.

Under Emperor Augustus, Rome had been consolidating its power in Germania through a series of campaigns aimed at expanding and securing control over the region, with the goal of establishing a stable province beyond the Rhine.

The Roman governor in the area, Publius Quinctilius Varus, was tasked with administering and pacifying the tribes, but his arrogance and overconfidence in their supposed loyalty would lead to his downfall.

The Roman forces under Varus numbered between 15,000 and 20,000 men, consisting of three legions (XVII, XVIII, and XIX), auxiliary cohorts, and a cavalry contingent.

These legions were experienced, well-trained, and disciplined, moving with the assurance of a force that believed in its unquestionable supremacy.

Varus's strategy relied on maintaining order through shows of strength and routine movements across the Germanic territories, without anticipating the possibility of a coordinated uprising.

The Roman legions were accompanied by a supply train and

civilians, which made their column long and vulnerable in the forested terrain.

On the opposing side, Arminius, leader of the Cherusci and trained in Roman military tactics through his service as an auxiliary in the Roman army, orchestrated a strategic and calculated rebellion.

Arminius exploited his deep understanding of Roman military operations to deceive Varus, convincing him that a minor uprising required his intervention beyond the secure limits.

Arminius's Germanic forces, numbering between 15,000 and 20,000 warriors from various allied tribes, consisted of light, agile infantry well-suited to the dense forests of Teutoburg.

Although they lacked sophisticated siege weapons, their intimate knowledge of the terrain proved to be a decisive advantage.

The trap was sprung as Varus and his legions advanced in a stretched-out and vulnerable formation through the Teutoburg Forest, a landscape marked by swampy ground and dense woodland, perfect for ambushes.

Adverse weather conditions, including heavy rain and fog, further reduced visibility and heightened confusion among the Roman ranks.

The legions' columns became even more elongated, and morale began to waver.

At that critical moment, Arminius, who had deserted shortly before under the guise of seeking reinforcements, launched his attack.

The Germans emerged from the trees and launched a surprise attack on the Romans, employing guerrilla tactics and avoiding direct hand-to-hand combat, which disoriented the legions that were unable to deploy properly.

The Romans attempted to form improvised defenses, but the terrain and the constant pressure from German assaults made it nearly impossible.

Temporary trenches and fortifications were quickly overwhelmed by the Germans, who struck from multiple directions.

The legionaries, with no room to maneuver and under a relentless rain of spears and arrows, began to fall into increasing disarray.

Arminius's use of ambushes, traps, and the fragmentation of Roman lines proved devastating.

For three days of sustained attacks, the Roman forces tried to break through and reorganize, but physical and psychological exhaustion, coupled with a lack of effective leadership, led to a massacre.

The Roman losses were staggering, with over 15,000 legionaries and auxiliaries killed or captured.

The legionary standards, symbols of honor and pride, were seized by the Germans—a devastating blow to Roman morale and a potent symbol of Arminius's victory.

Quintilius Varus, seeing the inevitable defeat, committed suicide to avoid capture—an act that became emblematic of the disaster and the horror of the defeat.

The consequences of the Battle of Teutoburg Forest were profound and far-reaching.

Rome, shocked and humiliated, abandoned its ambitions of expansion beyond the Rhine and strengthened its defenses along the frontier, marking the permanent boundary of the

Empire in that region for the remainder of its history.

Augustus, upon receiving the news, is said to have cried out in despair, "Varus, give me back my legions!"

Arminius solidified his status as a hero of Germanic resistance, though his victory also sowed discord among the tribes, which would eventually turn against each other.

The battle served as a stark reminder to Rome of the limits of its power and the constant challenges posed by frontier regions.

It shaped imperial strategy in the years and centuries that followed, prioritizing consolidation over unchecked expansion.

29

The Battle of Idistaviso

fought in 16 CE, was a decisive confrontation between the
Roman Empire and the Germanic tribes led by Arminius,
the same chieftain who had dealt Rome one of its greatest
defeats at the Battle of Teutoburg Forest.

Following the humiliating loss of three legions in that infamous
ambush in 9 CE, Rome had been compelled to strengthen its
defenses and rethink its strategies in the Germanic territories.

However, the desire for revenge and the need to restore
lost prestige drove Emperor Tiberius to dispatch General
Germanicus, one of the most talented commanders of the
era and grandnephew of Augustus, to lead a campaign of
retribution and demonstrate Rome's military might deep in
Germanic lands.

Germanicus commanded a formidable force of over 50,000
men, comprising eight core legions supported by auxiliary
cohorts and a substantial cavalry force, highlighting the
scale of Rome's effort to avenge the disgrace of Teutoburg.

Among these legions were battle-hardened veterans and
troops with extensive campaign experience, providing the
force with exceptional resilience and combat proficiency.

The auxiliary troops included archers, slingers, and Gallic
and Batavian cavalry, renowned for their loyalty and
battlefield prowess.

The Roman army was also equipped with light siege
engines and supply wagons, ensuring mobility and
sustained operations in hostile territory.

On the other side, the Germanic forces led by Arminius were a diverse coalition of allied tribes, including the Cherusci, Bructeri, and Marsii.

It is estimated that the Germans fielded a force of 40,000 to 50,000 warriors, comparable in size to the Roman army but lacking the cohesion and military discipline of the legions.

However, their knowledge of the terrain, mobility, and guerrilla tactics helped offset these disadvantages.

Arminius, having served as an auxiliary in the Roman army and familiar with its tactics and formations, was a cunning and charismatic leader who managed to inspire and unite the tribes in a common cause against Rome.

The battle took place in an area known as Idistaviso, near the Weser River, a vast plain surrounded by dense forests that offered the Germans the advantage of swift movement and concealment.

Determined to avoid the traps that had proven disastrous at Teutoburg, Germanicus deployed his legions in an open formation, with cavalry and auxiliaries positioned on the flanks and heavy infantry at the center.

This arrangement aimed to prevent ambushes and enable a swift response to any attacks from the surrounding woods.

The battle commenced as the Germans emerged from their positions among the trees, charging the Roman flanks with deafening war cries and characteristic ferocity.

The Roman cavalry, led by the Batavian units, repelled the initial assaults, holding the lines steady and preventing the Germans from breaking through the formation.

Arminius, aware of the need to fragment the Roman army, ordered lightning attacks at multiple points, aiming to disorganize and scatter the legions.

However, Germanicus had anticipated these tactics and instructed his officers to respond with coordinated maneuvers, including pincer movements and reinforcements from the rear.

The battle intensified as the Roman legionaries advanced in a testudo formation, shielding themselves under their interlocked shields from the Germanic projectiles.

The Roman pressure began to push the Germans toward the Weser River, where the terrain restricted their maneuverability.

Seeing the situation grow critical, Arminius led a final assault with his best warriors in a desperate effort to break through the Roman lines and regain the initiative.

The hand-to-hand combat was brutal, with Germanic warriors wielding swords and spears, while the legionaries responded with discipline and efficiency, using their gladii and pila.

Germanicus, understanding the symbolic importance of capturing or killing Arminius, directed his troops from a central position and ordered the cavalry to flank the Germanic warriors.

This strategic maneuver destabilized the Germans, who began to retreat in disarray.

The Germanic casualties were significant, with estimates of over 10,000 warriors killed on the battlefield, while Roman losses were smaller but still considerable, reflecting the prolonged engagement and the fierce resistance of the tribes.

At the end of the battle, the Germanic forces scattered, and Arminius managed to escape, but his prestige and the tribes' ability to continue fighting in a coordinated manner were severely diminished.

Victorious, Germanicus erected a trophy on the battlefield to commemorate the triumph and sent a clear message to Emperor Tiberius about the restoration of Roman honor.

The consequences of the Battle of Idistaviso temporarily consolidated Roman control and demonstrated the Empire's ability to recover from a monumental defeat.

However, they also reinforced Tiberius's decision to withdraw the legions and consolidate the borders along the Rhine, marking the end of Rome's major campaigns in Germania and establishing a policy of containment rather than expansion in the region.

30

The Battle of Watling Street

Fought in 61 AD, was a decisive confrontation between the Roman Empire and the forces of Queen Boudica, leader of the Iceni and a central figure in the rebellion against Roman occupation in Britannia.

This revolt arose as a result of the oppressive policies of the Roman procurator Catus Decianus and the brutal treatment of Boudica and her family following the death of her husband, Prasutagus, king of the Iceni.

Prasutagus had sought to secure the protection of his kingdom by dividing his inheritance between Rome and his daughters.

However, the Romans ignored his will, seizing the Iceni lands, looting their properties, and publicly humiliating Boudica by flogging her and violating her daughters.

This act of brutality ignited the fury of the Briton tribes, sparking a widespread uprising.

The Roman forces were led by Gaius Suetonius Paulinus, an experienced commander who had been engaged in a campaign on the island of Mona (modern-day Anglesey) to suppress Druidic resistance when the rebellion erupted.

Suetonius's army consisted of the Legio XIV Gemina and parts of the Legio XX Valeria Victrix, along with auxiliary troops and cavalry, totaling approximately 10,000 to 12,000 men.

These forces were highly trained, well-equipped, and accustomed to maintaining disciplined combat formations.

They wielded gladius swords, large shields (scutum), pilum (javelins), and were supported by armed cavalry.

Boudica, on the other hand, managed to assemble a vast army composed of tribes united under her leadership, including the Iceni, Trinovantes, and other groups from southeastern Britannia.

Her force is estimated to have numbered between 100,000 and 230,000 warriors, an impressive figure but consisting mostly of peasants armed with spears, clubs, short swords, and wooden shields.

Though they were numerous and driven by anger and a desire for revenge, they lacked the discipline and training of the Roman soldiers.

The battlefield chosen by Suetonius was a narrow plain bordered by dense forest along Watling Street, a strategic location that limited the possibility of an encircling attack by the Britons and forced their superior numbers to face the Roman army on a narrow front.

Suetonius positioned his legionaries in a classic formation, with heavy infantry in the center and auxiliary units and cavalry on the flanks, forming a solid line backed by the forest. This prevented retreat and strengthened their resolve to fight to the end.

The battle began with the war cries and a massive charge by the Britons, who advanced with fury, confident in their numerical superiority.

Boudica, riding her war chariot, led her troops, urging them to avenge the outrages they had suffered and to reclaim their freedom.

The Briton warriors advanced in a massive wave, seeking to overwhelm the Roman legions through sheer brute force.

However, the Roman legionaries waited patiently until the Britons were close enough before launching their pila, a volley of javelins that pierced the shields and bodies of the attackers, disorganizing their ranks.

This was followed by a coordinated charge of the Roman infantry, advancing in a wedge formation that penetrated the Briton lines and shattered their cohesion.

The Roman cavalry attacked the flanks, trapping the Britons and generating panic and confusion.

The battlefield turned into a bloody chaos as the Britons, caught between the Roman formations and their own war chariots blocking the rear, were unable to maneuver or retreat.

The narrow battlefield worked in favor of the Romans, who exploited their superior formation and weaponry to massacre the Britons.

Historical records indicate that Briton casualties were catastrophic, with figures ranging between 70,000 and 80,000 dead, while Roman losses were minimal, with fewer than 1,000 casualties.

The battle marked the end of Boudica's rebellion.

The queen, defeated and with no options left, retreated and, according to historians, took her own life to avoid capture.

Suetonius's victory secured Roman control over Britannia and demonstrated the unyielding power of the Roman Empire, consolidating the occupation and quelling large-scale uprisings for generations.

31

The Battle of Tapae

Fought in 88 AD, was a crucial confrontation between the Roman Empire, led by General Tettius Julianus under the orders of Emperor Domitian, and the forces of the Dacian Kingdom under King Decebalus.

This battle was part of the First Dacian War, a conflict that arose due to the constant incursions and threat posed by the Dacians to the Roman provinces along the Danube.

The Dacians, known for their martial prowess and ability to mobilize a formidable army, had become a persistent challenge to the stability and security of the Roman Empire.

The Roman army deployed at Tapae was a disciplined and well-equipped force comprising approximately 15,000 to 20,000 soldiers, including legionaries, auxiliaries, and cavalry units.

The legions prominent in the campaign included the Legio V Alaudae and Legio XIII Gemina, both veterans of multiple conflicts and well-trained in coordinated combat tactics.

The auxiliaries, drawn from various provinces, included archers, slingers, and light cavalry, while the heavy Roman cavalry bolstered the formation.

Additionally, the Romans were equipped with portable siege engines such as ballistae and scorpions, designed to hurl heavy projectiles and wreak havoc on enemy lines.

On the other hand, the Dacians, although fewer in number, mobilized an army of 12,000 to 15,000 men. Their infantry consisted of seasoned warriors wielding falcatas (curved swords), spears, and shields, renowned for their bravery and skill in close combat.

The Dacians also had formidable archers and slingers capable of harassing the enemy from a distance.

Their leader, Decebalus, was a cunning and courageous commander who knew the terrain well and employed guerrilla tactics and ambushes to offset the numerical and technological superiority of the Roman forces.

The battle took place in the Carpathian Mountains, on rugged terrain near the Tapae Pass, a strategic gateway into Dacia.

The mountainous environment, covered with dense forests and ravines, favored the Dacians' defensive and ambush strategies.

Tettius Julianus, aware of the challenges posed by the terrain, deployed his legions in compact formations, with auxiliaries and cavalry positioned on the flanks to prevent encirclement and siege engines ready to launch projectiles from the rear.

The engagement began as the Roman forces cautiously advanced through the Tapae Pass.

Decebalus, leveraging the terrain to his advantage, ordered a series of ambushes, with groups of warriors hidden among the trees and rocks.

The Dacians struck at the Roman vanguard, aiming to break their ranks and sow chaos.

Nevertheless, the discipline of the legionaries allowed them to withstand the initial assault.

The Romans quickly formed a shield wall and began advancing in phalanx formation, protecting themselves from the projectiles hurled by the Dacians from higher ground.

The battle intensified as the legions broke through the Dacians' first defensive line and pushed toward the center of their forces.

The Dacian infantry, led personally by Decebalus, fought fiercely, employing hit-and-run tactics to wear down the Roman troops.

Roman war machines began launching projectiles at the Dacian positions, inflicting significant casualties and breaking their morale.

The Roman cavalry, commanded by auxiliary officers, flanked the Dacian positions and attacked their supply lines, cutting off their retreat and sowing confusion.

The confrontation raged for hours, with heavy casualties on both sides.

Despite their losses, the Romans managed to maintain the cohesion of their ranks and pressed forward with determination.

Decebalus, realizing that his forces were being overwhelmed, ordered a strategic retreat to preserve what remained of his army and avoid total annihilation.

The Dacians withdrew to the mountains, leaving the battlefield in Roman hands but managing to save a significant portion of their forces to fight in future campaigns.

Roman casualties were estimated at around 3,000 soldiers, including legionaries and auxiliaries, while Dacian losses were higher, with at least 5,000 warriors killed or wounded.

Despite the victory, the Romans were unable to fully capitalize on their success due to the challenging terrain and Decebalus' ability to reorganize his forces in the mountains.

The Battle of Tapae, though a tactical victory for the Romans, did not result in the definitive conquest of Dacia.

However, it demonstrated the resilience of the Dacians and underscored the need for a more comprehensive and organized campaign.

Upon receiving news of the victory, Domitian used it to bolster his political position in Rome, though he remained aware that Decebalus would continue to pose a latent threat.

The battle laid the groundwork for future campaigns, including Trajan's expedition, which ultimately led to the conquest of Dacia in 106 A.D.

32

The Battle of Ctesiphon.

Fought in 198 AD, it was a pivotal clash between the Roman Empire, led by Emperor Septimius Severus, and the Parthian Empire under King Vologases V.

This conflict was part of the Roman-Parthian Wars, a series of intermittent military campaigns between these two powerful empires over control of Mesopotamia and Armenia.

After consolidating his power in Rome following a period of civil war, Septimius Severus launched a campaign in the East to expand Roman influence and assert his authority through a demonstration of military might.

The Roman army that Severus led into the campaign consisted of approximately 30,000 to 40,000 soldiers.

It included several veteran legions, such as the Legio XIV Gemina and the Legio I Parthica, which Severus had specifically created for his eastern campaigns.

Additionally, he was supported by auxiliaries from various regions of the empire: horse archers from Thrace, light infantry, lancers, and heavy cavalry.

He also brought a significant contingent of siege engines, including catapults, battering rams, and ballistae, which would prove crucial in the siege of Ctesiphon, the Parthian Empire's capital.

The Parthian forces, numbering approximately 20,000 to 30,000 men, included their feared cataphract cavalry, renowned for their full-body armor and devastating charges.

The Parthians also fielded horse archers, masters of hit-and-run tactics, which made it difficult for the Romans to sustain prolonged direct engagements.

Vologases V, aware of the formidable power of the Roman legions, placed his confidence in the fortifications of Ctesiphon and the city's ability to withstand a prolonged siege.

The siege of Ctesiphon began with the Roman legions advancing toward the fortified city.

Severus divided his forces into columns to encircle the city and cut off its supply lines.

The Romans established fortified camps around the city and prepared their siege engines.

Ballistae and catapults hurled stones and fire projectiles at Ctesiphon's walls, aiming to weaken the defenses and sow chaos within the city.

The Roman infantry remained in tight formations to repel the relentless attacks of the cataphract cavalry, which sought to break the siege and disrupt Roman supply lines.

At night, Parthian archers launched swift and effective raids, harassing Roman troops and inflicting significant casualties.

However, Severus ordered his infantry archers and auxiliaries to retaliate with volleys of arrows, creating a crossfire that kept the Parthian skirmishers at bay.

At dawn, the legions advanced methodically with battering rams and siege towers, seeking breaches in the walls to launch a frontal assault.

The Romans employed mining tactics to undermine the walls and weaken their foundations, while military engineers constructed assault ramps to facilitate entry into the city.

The battle reached its climax when the Romans successfully breached the walls of Ctesiphon.

Severus ordered a massive charge of heavy infantry and auxiliaries, who stormed through the breach and faced fierce resistance from the Parthian defenders.

Fighting within the city's streets was intense, with brutal hand-to-hand combat resulting in heavy casualties on both sides.

The Romans, better trained and numerically superior at this critical moment, slowly pushed toward the city's core.

The Parthian cataphracts attempted to regroup for a final charge, but the lack of space and narrow streets hindered their ability to unleash their full strength.

The resistance in Ctesiphon crumbled as the Romans captured key strategic points, including the main gate and the central plaza.

Vologases V and his court managed to escape before the city fully fell into Severus' hands, avoiding capture.

Roman casualties were estimated at approximately 5,000 to 7,000 men—a significant loss but manageable given the scale of the victory.

The Parthians suffered heavier losses, with at least 10,000 soldiers killed or captured, and the city was sacked, yielding substantial spoils that Severus used to fund future campaigns and reward his troops.

The consequences of the Battle of Ctesiphon were far-reaching.

Although the city was plundered and Severus' prestige greatly enhanced, the victory did not result in the permanent annexation of Parthian territories.

The continued resistance of Vologases V and the logistical challenges of maintaining sustained control over Mesopotamia eventually forced the Romans to withdraw.

Nevertheless, the expedition bolstered Severus' image as a conquering emperor and solidified his power in Rome, demonstrating his ability to lead the Empire in successful campaigns both in the East and West.

The temporary fall of Ctesiphon showcased Rome's capacity to besiege and capture one of the most formidable cities of the ancient world, marking a significant milestone in the historical rivalry between Rome and the Parthians.

33

The Battle of Adrianople

Fought in 378 AD, was a pivotal event in the history of the Roman Empire and one of the most catastrophic defeats it ever suffered.

This battle took place in the context of the massive migration of Gothic peoples into Roman territory, a process that began when the Goths, pressured by the advancing Huns, sought refuge in Roman lands across the Danube River.

Emperor Valens, ruler of the Eastern Roman Empire, agreed to allow the Goths to settle in his territories on the condition that they swear loyalty and submit to Roman control.

However, the corruption of local officials, who abused and exploited the Goths, along with severe shortages of food and supplies, created a climate of tension and unrest that quickly escalated into open rebellion.

Valens' Roman army comprised approximately 15,000 to 20,000 soldiers, including heavy infantry legions, light cavalry, and auxiliary units drawn from various regions of the empire.

These troops were well-trained, but internal tensions and a lack of cohesive leadership undermined their effectiveness.

Eager to secure a swift victory to bolster his prestige and prevent the intervention of Emperor Gratian of the Western Roman Empire, Valens decided to engage the Goths without waiting for additional reinforcements.

The Goths, led by Fritigern, had a force of approximately 20,000 to 25,000 warriors, including heavy infantry, archers, and a significant cavalry contingent, which included allied barbarian tribes.

The Goths had established a strategic position near Adrianople, setting up a fortified camp surrounded by wagons and other improvised barriers to protect their women and children.

This defensive tactic also allowed them to control the terrain and await reinforcements from allied tribes.

The battle commenced when Valens, underestimating the strength of the Goths and overestimating the capabilities of his own troops, decided to attack the Gothic camp without waiting for Gratian's arrival.

The Roman legions advanced in formation, organized into cohorts maintaining a tight front.

Valens, positioned on a nearby hill, directed the battle from an elevated vantage point, confident that his heavy infantry could break through the Gothic lines and crush Fritigern's resistance.

However, the Goths, aware of the Roman army's approach, employed a clever strategy.

Fritigern sent messengers to Valens under the pretense of negotiating peace, buying time for the Gothic cavalry reinforcements, which were out on a reconnaissance mission, to return.

The tactic succeeded; as the Romans held their formation, Gothic cavalry reinforcements suddenly appeared on the right flank of the Roman army.

The Gothic cavalry's attack was devastating, catching the Roman cavalry off guard and forcing them into a disorganized retreat.

The Roman infantry, surrounded and attacked from both the front and the flanks, found itself trapped in a deadly encirclement.

The Goths, now numerically superior at this critical moment, began to advance with overwhelming force.

The Romans fought bravely, but the confusion and lack of clear leadership caused their resistance to collapse rapidly.

The Gothic assault was relentless.

The Roman infantry, unable to break the encirclement, was crushed in a massacre that lasted for hours.

The soldiers, trapped and with no room to maneuver, fell in great numbers, unable to organize an effective retreat.

Valens, realizing the scale of the defeat, attempted to coordinate a withdrawal but was overtaken by the Goths and perished on the battlefield, likely burned alive in a house where he had sought refuge.

Roman casualties were catastrophic, estimated at 10,000 to 15,000 men, a devastating loss for the Empire.

The Goths also suffered significant losses, though fewer, due to their ability to employ mobile tactics and coordinated attacks that maximized their effectiveness while minimizing casualties.

The consequences of the Battle of Adrianople were far-reaching.

The death of Emperor Valens and the destruction of a significant portion of the Eastern Roman army left the Eastern Roman Empire vulnerable and without effective leadership.

This defeat marked the beginning of a period of weakening in in Rome's military and political power, and many historians view it as a harbinger of the eventual fall of the Western Empire in the centuries to come.

The battle also demonstrated that the Roman armies were no longer invincible and that barbarian forces, when well-led and organized, could inflict serious damage on the empire.

34

The Battle of the Catalaunian Plains

Fought in 451 AD, was one of the most significant clashes during the decline of the Roman Empire and one of the last attempts by the empire to reassert its power against a devastating foreign threat.

By the 5th century, the Western Roman Empire was in crisis due to internal and external pressures.

The administration was fragile, and central authority had been weakened by the growing influence of military leaders and the incursions of various barbarian tribes invading Roman territory.

In this context, Attila, the king of the Huns, had emerged as a formidable threat.

Known as the "Scourge of God," Attila had consolidated his power over a vast empire stretching from Central Europe to the borders of the Byzantine Empire.

With his mobile warfare tactics and ability to instill terror, Attila launched a campaign of plunder and conquest that threatened to overrun Gaul.

The Roman army, under the leadership of General Flavius Aetius, known as the last great Roman general, faced a monumental task.

Aetius, with a sharp understanding of the need to forge alliances, managed to assemble a mixed army composed not only of the remaining Roman legions but also of forces from various allied tribes, including the Visigoths led by King Theodoric I, as well as Alans and Franks.

In total, Aetius' allied force is estimated to have numbered between 50,000 and 80,000 men.

The troops included heavy Roman infantry, elite Visigothic cavalry, Alanic horsemen, and auxiliary contingents.

Despite facing an internal crisis with limited Roman resources, Aetius skillfully leveraged temporary loyalties to create a united front against the Huns.

Attila commanded an army estimated to be between 60,000 and 100,000 men, according to some sources.

His forces were a mix of mounted Hunnic warriors, renowned for their composite bows and expertise in rapid assaults, as well as auxiliary soldiers from subjugated Germanic tribes and other allies, including the Ostrogoths and Gepids.

The Huns were masters of guerrilla tactics, capable of launching swift raids and retreats to disorient the enemy before delivering devastating attacks.

The battlefield, located on the vast, rolling plains of the Catalaunian Fields (modern-day Chalons-en-Champagne, France), was ideal for cavalry, favoring both the Huns and the Visigoths.

Both sides prepared for a confrontation that would determine the future of Gaul and, to a large extent, that of the Western Roman Empire.

On the day of the battle, Aetius strategically deployed his forces.

The central line was held by heavy Roman infantry and Alanic contingents, who were positioned to absorb the anticipated frontal assault from Attila.

The Visigoths, led by Theodoric, were positioned on the right flank, prepared to protect the most vulnerable side and deliver a decisive charge at the opportune moment.

On the left flank, Aetius placed the Franks and other allied tribes, who would reinforce the position and respond to enemy maneuvers.

Attila, meanwhile, positioned his mounted archers in the center, ready to unleash a storm of arrows on the enemy lines.

The infantry of his Germanic allies and the most seasoned Hunnic warriors were stationed on the flanks, poised to execute an enveloping assault.

The battle began with a volley of arrows fired by the Huns, wreaking havoc on the front lines of the Roman and Alanic infantry.

However, Aetius, well aware of Attila's tactical prowess, ordered his men to hold their formation.

In response, the Roman infantry advanced steadily, absorbing the initial charge and allowing the Visigoths to launch a counterattack from the right flank.

The Visigothic cavalry, renowned for its powerful charges, advanced with great force, breaking through Attila's auxiliary lines and sowing confusion.

The fighting was fierce and chaotic.

Amid the battle's turmoil, Theodoric, the Visigothic king, fell in combat—a severe blow to the morale of his people.

Nevertheless, his sons took command, and with renewed fury, they drove the Hunnic forces back.

Attila, seeing his forces beginning to retreat and the battle taking a dangerous turn, ordered a strategic withdrawal into his fortified camp, hoping to regroup and launch a renewed attack the following day.

The battle ended with heavy losses on both sides.

It is estimated that at least 15,000 to 20,000 soldiers perished on the battlefield.

The Roman and Visigothic alliance managed to hold the field, forcing Attila to retreat without achieving a decisive victory.

The consequences of the Battle of the Catalaunian Plains were significant.

Although Attila survived and retained his power, the Huns' reputation for invincibility was challenged for the first time, proving they could be stopped.

For the Western Roman Empire, the costly victory, while not eliminating the long-term threat, allowed Aetius to consolidate his position as Rome's defender.

However, internal tensions and power struggles continued to weaken the empire, paving the way for its eventual fall in the following decades.

The Visigoths, though wounded by the loss of their king, emerged stronger and gained greater respect as a power within Gaul.

The battle is remembered as a rare example of cooperation between Romans and barbarian tribes, a final display of Roman military prowess against the forces that would ultimately reshape Europe.

35

The Battle of Ravenna

Took place in 476 AD and marked a pivotal moment in the
history of the Western Roman Empire, as it preceded its
ultimate collapse.

In the context of the 5th century, the Western Roman Empire
faced a profound crisis, characterized by unprecedented
political and military weakness.

Emperor Romulus Augustulus, considered the last emperor
of the Western Roman Empire, was barely a teenager with no
real power, while his father, Flavius Orestes, acted as regent
and the true ruler of the throne.

In contrast, the Eastern Roman Empire, under stronger
emperors and a more centralized administration, maintained
a degree of stability.

However, in the West, the situation was dire, with a
fragmented territory constantly threatened by invasions
and rebellions from various barbarian tribes.

In 476 AD, Odoacer, a Germanic military leader and chief of
the Heruli tribe, emerged as a key contender.

Odoacer had gathered a coalition of Germanic tribes and
mercenary elements serving under the Roman banner but
disgruntled by the lack of pay and unequal treatment.

These Germanic forces included Heruli, Sciri, and Rugii,
forming a contingent of approximately 20,000 men.

Although most of these soldiers were experienced infantry
warriors, there were also detachments of light cavalry skilled

in swift and fierce combat tactics.

Odoacer, known for his charismatic leadership and ability to forge alliances, led these forces.

On the other hand, Flavius Orestes had consolidated an army comprising the remnants of the Roman legions in northern Italy, bolstered by loyal auxiliary troops.

These forces were mostly heavy infantry, though their numbers were inferior to Odoacer's, estimated at between 10,000 and 15,000 men.

The Roman infantry still retained some of its legendary discipline, though morale was weakened by years of defeats and lack of pay.

The Roman cavalry, once an essential component of the imperial forces, was reduced to a few hundred riders, insufficient to counter the barbarian threat.

The battlefield was chosen near the city of Ravenna, which by then had replaced Rome as the capital of the Western Empire due to its more defensible location and natural fortifications surrounded by swamps and rivers.

However, its proximity to the sea and limited supplies worked against Orestes' forces, who faced a motivated barbarian coalition determined to crush Roman resistance once and for all.

The battle began at dawn, with Odoacer ordering his archers and slingers to unleash a barrage of projectiles on the Roman lines.

This was followed by a charge from Odoacer's Germanic infantry, attacking in waves to break through the first Roman defensive line.

Orestes, aware of his numerical disadvantage, had placed his best men at the center, while the flanks were reinforced with auxiliary troops and reservists.

The Roman infantry valiantly held their ground, using their shields to block the barrage of arrows and maintaining a tight formation.

However, Odoacer employed a flanking maneuver, sending his light cavalry to attack the Roman flanks and destabilize their lines.

The barbarians roared with relentless fervor, and soon the pressure on Orestes' weakened flanks began to take effect.

Despite efforts to maintain cohesion, the Roman auxiliary troops started to fall back, creating gaps that the Germanic warriors quickly exploited.

The close combat was brutal and prolonged.

The Roman soldiers, trained in orderly combat techniques, tried to hold their formation, but the numerical superiority and ferocity of the barbarians overwhelmed them.

The Roman cavalry made a desperate attempt to counterattack and relieve the pressure on the center, but they were quickly repelled by Odoacer's light cavalry and well-positioned auxiliary infantry.

The turning point came when Orestes was captured while attempting to reorganize his forces and fend off a Germanic advance on the right flank.

With the capture of their leader, the morale of the Roman troops collapsed, and the army disintegrated.

Roman casualties were high, estimated at least 7,000 to 9,000 men, while Odoacer's forces also suffered significant losses, with around 4,000 dead and wounded, but maintained control of the battlefield.

The capture and subsequent execution of Orestes marked the end of organized resistance by the Western Roman Empire.

Odoacer marched on Ravenna and deposed Romulus Augustulus, who, being too young and powerless, was exiled rather than executed.

This symbolic act marked the formal collapse of the Western Roman Empire.

Roman authority in the West was replaced by the rule of barbarian kings, and Odoacer declared himself King of Italy, sending the imperial insignia to Constantinople as a signal that there was no longer an emperor in the West.

The consequences of the Battle of Ravenna were profound.

It not only signified the fall of the Western Roman Empire but also ushered in an era of fragmentation and political reconfiguration in Europe, where former Roman territories became kingdoms ruled by Germanic leaders.

The battle marked the end of over a thousand years of Roman dominance, leaving a legacy that would shape European culture, politics, and history for centuries to come.

Made in the USA
Columbia, SC
06 December 2024

48593785R00076